RELIGION
POLITICS AND
THE HIGHER
LEARNING

BOOKS BY MORTON WHITE

Religion, Politics, and the Higher Learning

Toward Reunion in Philosophy

The Age of Analysis (ed.)

Social Thought in America: The Revolt Against Formalism

The Origin of Dewey's Instrumentalism

RELIGION POLITICS AND THE HIGHER LEARNING

A Collection of Essays

MORTON WHITE

HARVARD UNIVERSITY PRESS

CAMBRIDGE · MASSACHUSETTS

1959

Distributed in Great Britain by Oxford University Press, London

Library of Congress Catalog Card No. 59-6163

Printed in the United States of America

TO

NICHOLAS AND STEPHEN

Preface

THE word 'philosophy' is both old and ambiguous — in fact, ambiguous because it is so old. It may mean 'love of wisdom' in the original Greek, but to the professional student it is a formidably technical subject which is divided into its four departments of logic, metaphysics, theory of knowledge, and ethics. Expertise in these departments requires neither wisdom nor love of wisdom, not even expertise in ethics when it is thought of simply as the analysis of moral concepts. In the past the philosopher was supposed to be, among other things, both a logician and a sage. He reflected on the nature of inference and was expected to deliver wise sayings on moral, political, and social problems. But today, especially in England and America, the philosophy of life and the philosophy of civilization are often regarded as disreputable Continental concerns, hardly to be called subjects in the academic sense. Political philosophy, we are told by one British don, is dead. Another has remarked on the slump in sages. The philosophy of history, or what is left of it, has been cheerfully surrendered to historians and sociologists, and the philosophy of education has been returned with a sigh of relief to normal schools. Parts of philosophy which have been most closely connected with the pressing problems of ordinary men have either been destroyed or disowned, sometimes by philosophers who say that they do so the better to deal with the words of ordinary men. Is it surprising then that some of these abandoned problems should find eager foster-parents outside of professional philosophy? Difficulties that are not to darken the doors of technically trained philosophers are welcomed at the doors of dark philosophers.

All of the great philosophers before John Stuart Mill dealt with basic problems of western civilization, as Mill did, of course. Descartes urged the necessity of applying reason in all departments of human life; Locke supplied one of the most striking expositions of the doctrine of natural law that underlies so much of western legal thinking; Hume provided one of the most penetrating analyses of the arguments for the existence of God; Rousseau set the tone of educational theory for over a century; Kant brought modern philosophy to a climax with a doctrine that profoundly treated science, religion, art, and morals; Hegel searched for the spirit of history; John Stuart Mill tried to apply traditional British empiricism to the central political and cultural problems of British life. But as soon as we leave Hegel and Mill in the nineteenth century and continue a historically arranged search for illumination on matters of general concern we do not often find ourselves reading philosophers in the technically minded professional's sense of that term. More often the writers we read are *penseurs*, *littérateurs*, theologians, politicians, psychoanalysts, sociologists, or journalists. We enter the swirling currents created by Marx, Dostoevsky, Kierkegaard, Nietzsche, and Freud, currents that swerve sharply from the mainstream of modern philosophy.

Part of what has happened, I suggest, is that the more recent legatees of the great tradition in western philosophy have, by their own indifference to certain human questions, created a philosophical vacuum into which the *penseurs* and their disciples have rushed. I do not mean to denigrate those thinkers who shoulder a job that is big enough for philosophy but too big for philosophers in England and America. My aim is more positive. I want to direct an appeal to those who have inherited the problems and transformed the techniques of traditional philosophy. I hope that they will revive their interest in subjects like the philosophy of law, of politics, of education, of religion, and of history without surrendering their interest in the more remote questions of ethics, epistemology, logic, and metaphysics, and without sacrificing the exacting standards of these other disciplines. Such a hope is not excessively utopian and I wish to make a contribution, however small, to its fulfillment in this book. There are many signs that the sleeping giant of philosophy is arousing itself out of its mathematical slumbers. Both here and in Britain one can detect the rebirth of rigorous humanism, especially among younger philosophers who have come to realize that there are languages other than those of formal logic and natural science.

With this in mind I have gathered together a number of pieces which have been addressed to the general reader in the last seven or eight years. I have revised them with an eye to improving them and linking them more closely together, and the result is, I believe, a unified book of essays. It consists of an introductory plea for greater philosophic interest in the problems of history, education, politics, law, and religion; a group of essays in which certain tendencies and techniques of recent philosophy are described; and a group of essays which deal philosophically with a few serious problems confronting the student of, and the participant in, western society in the twentieth century. Although the essays seem to me best organized in this manner, no one of them presupposes a knowledge of any other, and therefore the reader is advised to take any path through them which he finds illuminating or interesting.

For their permission to reprint I wish to thank the editors and publishers of periodicals in which previously printed pieces have appeared. As always, my wife, Lucia Perry White, has been a constant source of help and loving encouragement. She has read every one of the essays and has made invaluable suggestions about the final form of this volume.

MORTON WHITE
June 1958

Contents

RELIGION

POLITICS AND

THE HIGHER

LEARNING

I •

The Social Role of Philosophy

THE last thirty years or so have witnessed a slow and silent revolution in philosophy which has gone almost unnoticed by the layman. It has been part of its program to insist on the technical character of philosophical investigation and on the fact that philosophy cannot be carried on irresponsibly and pompously; it has said good-bye forever to the days of the fat, two-volumed *Weltanschauung*. Let those who yearn for those days try to read one of the classics of the glistering age of American philosophy — for example, Royce's *The World and the Individual* — and they will see why the era of speculative metaphysics has lost its charm for the young American philosopher. The young American philosopher has become more and more absorbed in analytic philosophy, under which a variety of different doctrines are included, some of them positivistic and others decidedly antipositivistic in character. The temper and tone of the movement is deflationary and critical; its method linguistic and logical. While some of its sponsors emphasize the importance of reconstructing ordinary language, others insist on the need for describing the behavior of words as ordinarily used. What they all oppose, however, is the pretentious method of those who claim to conduct us to the Truth by way of labyrinthine metaphysical systems, aided by the flimsiest threads.

This revolution has a highly respectable philosophical ancestry in spite of the concerted efforts to discredit it as philistine. The names of Locke, Hume, Bentham, and Mill attest to that, but they also attest to a fundamental difference between philosophy as conceived by earlier empiricists and philosophy as conceived by their contemporary successors. Their successors have virtually abandoned all of the more humane philosophical disciplines. When one thinks of Locke's *Two Treatises of Government*, Mill's *On Liberty*, and even Hume's *History*, one sees by contrast how narrow the empiricist tradition has become. The need for specialization, the need to probe more deeply into fundamental questions of logic and epistemology has robbed most analytic philosophers of the time, energy, and inclination to think about social, political, and moral problems. They venture into mathematics and physics when stimulated by logical needs, and flirt with psychology in the theory of knowledge, but most of their finely ground axes have been used to sharpen other axes. Few of the redwoods of human concern ever fall before them.

This loss of touch with cultural and political questions is one of the most striking features of Anglo-American philosophy in the last generation and it constitutes one of the most unfortunate concomitants of a brilliant period in the history of philosophy. While Marxists and Existentialists carry their street-corner battles into the university and beyond, the ablest Englishmen and Americans treat social philosophy, political philosophy, and the philosophy of history as disreputable subjects which are worthy only of geniuses and charlatans. This attitude has developed to such an extent that even those who do metaphysics in desperate imitation of the grand manner no longer act out their dreams in social and political treatises but rather content themselves with using low-powered logic on traditional technical problems in an essentially quixotic way. There is some interest in esthetics, of course, but this frequently results in monstrosities which are rightly ignored by all who have any feeling for the arts and literature.

The philosophical drift away from the humane disciplines has been made more dramatic by the fact that the American intellectual and the American college and university are more than ever searching for some kind of philosophical credo. This is reflected not only in the rebirth of academic interest in theology and religion, but also in the spread of the idea of General Education. Everywhere in the social sciences and humanities one finds a thirst for philosophy, and in just as many places one finds disappointment with professional philosophers. The immediate result is twofold: on the one hand a lamentable development of philosophical pretentiousness among journalists, sociologists, historians, and physicists; on the other, too many dry, insensitive farmer-philosophers, ignorant of the sciences, indifferent to the history of their own discipline, and lacking feeling for matters of human concern. Among the amateur philosophers there is more undisciplined talk than ever on the problem of value, on the patterns of history, on the nature and destiny of man; and among the professionals a growing sense of embattlement while defending their inalienable right to talk only about sense-data, implication, and the synthetic *a priori*.

This is the disturbing situation which faces the philosopher who wants to work in the great tradition of logical analysis without cutting himself off from the equally great tradition of social criticism, the man who rightly remembers that Locke on property and Mill on liberty are easily as important as Locke on real essences and Mill on the syllogism. His situation reflects a larger problem: How can serious, technical philosophers honorably regain that position of leadership and respect among intellectuals and the general public which has slowly slipped from their hands?

It should be said very quickly that philosophers will not buy this position. They will not sacrifice their right to investigate the most recondite technical questions; they will not cease writing for the *Journal of Symbolic Logic* and *Mind* in order to devote themselves exclusively to Sunday-supplement scholarship. And so the problem becomes one of uniting an interest in analysis with an interest in social and political affairs. It needn't be a matter of every mathematical logician producing an axiomatized charter of human rights. Some of us are old enough to remember how Marxism pressured the American intellectual of the thirties into jobs for which he had no talent, and all of us are old enough to see the dangers of widespread intellectual Lysenkoism. It is rather a matter of living a life which is not spiritually and intellectually torn, since double roles in this instance can never lead to anything but double talk. There are those who can divide their lives with ease, much as some people play both the piano and the violin, but the philosopher is usually driven by a need for consistency and integrity; if he plays more than one instrument he is more likely to be a one-man band than to double in brass.

One way to bring about this unity is to encourage the young philosophical analyst to dig his honest and sharp instruments into those places which have so often been the lairs of charlatanry and obscurantism. While responsible philosophers have worked soberly and intensively in metaphysics, logic, and epistemology, the forum has been filled with wild talk on value, history, democracy, human rights, and liberal education. But if only a tiny part of the philosophical energy and clearheadedness which have gone into logic had been devoted to clarification of the issues which surround social and political questions, we might find ourselves closer to the solution of some of our pressing problems.

There is one serious misunderstanding which must be identified and avoided. It would be a mistake to construe this suggestion as another example of philosophical pretentiousness, an expression of the view that philosophy is a lordly discipline which, if it should only decide to turn seriously to social questions, would produce all the answers. We must also avoid a philosophical myth about philosophy, unfortunately sponsored by too many analytic philosophers, according to which philosophy aspires to a higher kind of knowledge than that which the ordinary man and scientist can attain. On this view philosophy consists of necessary propositions which are impervious to the demands of experience according to some and indifferent to the demands of scientific convenience according to others. Fortunately this myth is being challenged successfully by analytic philosophers themselves, so that they need no longer defend in modish language an essentially outmoded conception of their task. Philosophy may be more abstract than empirical science and the ordinary man's knowledge, and it may be especially concerned with definitions and descriptions of linguistic behavior, but the process whereby it justifies the acceptance of these definitions and descriptions is not radically different from that which goes on in science and ordinary life. For this reason philosophers should approach the problems of law, political science, and history, not with the idea that they are supplying a method that is absolutely foreign to what already goes on in those disciplines, but rather with the idea that they are carrying out more carefully and self-consciously what is an acknowledged part of the process of inquiry. On these terms their cooperation with workers in other fields will be genuine and not a matter of pompous philosophical dignitaries stooping to conquer all of the difficulties which elude the ingenuity of lawyers and politicians.

What I have been advocating so far will seem insufficient to some, for it amounts to nothing more than getting clear about the fundamental terms of social and political discourse. This is more of the same logomachy and scholasticism, it will be said. What we want from philosophers is a substantive ethic, not a series of abstract definitions that leave us just as far as ever from a solution of our practical problems. Now in spite of the childishness of expecting philosophers to produce dreary systems of ethical rules, there is a certain justice in this attitude. It serves to warn us of its equally absurd opposite, the view that philosophers are forbidden by the very definition of their calling to be concerned with the substantive problems of moral criticism. This is the killing formalism which often takes hold of lively movements. It is the attitude of analytic philosophers who leave moral criticism to those whom they call "moralists" or to social scientists who are just as anxious to palm off the job on somebody else. In this passing of the ethical buck one can observe the preoccupation with a rigid classification of the sciences, the unproductive, scholastic division of the intellectual globe.

"Here ends philosophy," say the constables of the intellect, "and you shall go no farther." The result has been a progressive narrowing of the scope of philosophy, with bloodless analysts doing their jobs on one side of the barrier, forbidden by the definition of their subject from engaging in cultural criticism. But when Locke spoke out against the divine right of kings, and Bentham against the legal outrages of his day, and Mill on liberty, they did not think they were entering a field sharply separated from philosophy. They were interested in the substantive questions which illustrated and gave practical significance to their efforts at analysis. And just this interest in the practical consequences of their analyses made them intellectual leaders of their age. A similar combination of interests has made Bertrand Russell and John Dewey great men in our own time. How can a moral philosopher test his analyses except by seeing how they square with political and ethical judgments that we make or are likely to make? It will be said, I know, that philosophy is the analysis of concepts and that we can know that the concept of man is identical with the concept of rational animal without ever examining a single man or knowing just who is or what isn't a man. But this is another legacy of an outmoded view of philosophical analysis.

One task of political philosophy is the clarification of fundamental words like 'liberty', 'democracy', and 'equality', but the success of such an effort at clarification is to be measured partly by examining its significance for concrete political judgments and action. Any definition of 'democracy' which leads us to say that Soviet Russia is a democracy is obviously an absurd definition. And it is grotesque to say here with Humpty-Dumpty that we can define words as we choose, or that

Russia is a democracy "on Stalin's definition." The philosopher's need to accept or reject concrete ethical judgments flows directly from the fact that he can only test the adequacy of his analyses by checking them against the moral convictions which he and others share. The philosopher's responsibility is analogous to that of the empirical scientist, except that the empirical scientist is more concerned with checking his theories against the evidence of the senses. The view that the relation between philosophical definitions and the language which they explicate is fundamentally different from the relation between scientific theories and the observed facts which they explain is another manifestation of the untenable dualism between the analytic and the synthetic which has dominated so much philosophy. In the case of ethics and political philosophy it is responsible for much of the self-imposed helplessness which some philosophers feel in the presence of social questions.

I am not urging that every philosopher turn himself into a full-time moral judge. Any philosopher who prefers the peace and quiet of mathematical set-theory to practical ethics is welcome to it, and I hope the day will never come when a social or political tithe is exacted from those who cherish a life devoted to epistemology. What I am urging is that special interest in social and political problems need not constitute an abandonment of philosophy, and that those philosophers who choose to clarify or analyze social, political, and moral discourse must be familiar with the facts of political and social life. Moreover they will enrich and improve their analytic work if they are familiar with those facts, not as a disengaged anthropologist knows the convictions of his primitives or as a psychoanalyst knows the fears of his patients, but rather in a more direct and personal way. Such direct and personal knowledge can come with being engaged in social and cultural affairs. It need not mean abandonment of the calmness which is demanded by analysis, any more than looking robs an astronomer of the power to theorize.

I have made two pleas so far. The first is for greater analytic interest in social and political ideas, in the description and understanding of culture and politics. This will not involve a fundamental change in the method of analytic philosophy; it will merely add to its subject matter. Of course the enormous growth of our knowledge about society and politics since the days of Locke and Mill will make it impossible for a philosopher to go it alone. He will need training in history and in the social sciences like that which a philosopher of physics must have in physics. My second plea is more controversial because it calls for a greater concern with normative ethics than is fashionable among analytic thinkers today. Here I am not merely asking for an extension of the method of analysis to a neglected subject matter but rather for a realization of the fact that the line between the analytic and the synthetic is so blurred as to make it virtually impossible for an analyst of ethical notions to avoid being seriously concerned with the substantive questions of personal and social ethics. Furthermore, the prevailing notion that there is a set of specialists who are "moralists" and who therefore make it unnecessary for philosophers to treat moral questions seriously has opened the door to frauds and fools. The questions of substantive ethics are questions for all men; they should never become the private domain of moralists. If they do, one of the priceless legacies of western civilization will have been lost to the Grand Inquisitor.

As if he were writing in order to confirm one's gloomiest views of the future, a recent writer asks: "Is the intellectual obsolete?" * and propounds an answer which is in striking opposition to the point of view for which I have been contending. A "freely speculating mind or intellectual," he says, is one who seeks the truth and who follows the argument wherever it may lead, whereas a "mental technician" is a practical mind who serves a party, a leader, or a government so slavishly that he surrenders the right to criticize their aims and methods. The mental technician on this view may exercise ingenuity and skill in achieving the aims set for him by his employer or leader but he is, in the last analysis, a slave. We are given the impression that there is no mean between these two extremes and we are given to understand that the kind of free, practical philosophy for which I have been pleading is hopelessly out of date.

Now I have no doubt that there are many people who fit into one or the other of these neatly carved categories, but it seems to me that a third kind of "brain worker" is being squeezed out of the picture in an effort to simplify the past and future of the intellectual. I mean the man who uses his wits in an effort to further practical aims of which he approves, which he periodically re-examines, and which he feels free to reject whenever experience, feeling, or reflection lead to such a conclusion. This third type of individual is the nearest thing in the intellectual world to a free, rational, whole

* See an article by Stuart Hughes bearing this title in *Commentary*, October 1956. The remarks that follow are an adaptation of a response to Professor Hughes in the January 1957 issue of *Commentary*.

human being. He is neither a metaphysician nor an apparatus-man. His interests fall between those of the speculative philosopher and those of the technician. He will not be obsolete so long as the ideal of the free man survives. He differs from the "freely speculating mind" in the degree to which he addresses himself to practical questions, and from the servile mental technician because of his refusal to sell himself into intellectual slavery.

Intellectuals are more likely to secure the kind of influence whose disappearance is lamented, not by writing on Gödel's theorem, on the ontological argument, or on the synthetic *a priori*, but rather by dealing with questions of more immediate human concern. These are rarely "speculative questions" in the traditional sense. Locke's *Essay Concerning Human Understanding* was written by the man who wrote the *Second Treatise of Civil Government* in defense of the Whig cause. His political influence arose from having defended that cause. Mill's essay *On Liberty* was the main medium of his great influence as an "intellectual," and not his *Examination of Sir William Hamilton's Philosophy*, which was addressed to specialists in epistemology. It was Bentham on legal outrages, and not Bentham on the theory of fictions, who assumed a role so rarely assumed by philosophers today. The lamentable fact of our intellectual life today is not the disappearance of the purely speculative thinker, for he continues to exist in profusion in universities throughout the United States. What we should be worried about is the disappearance of that in-between thinker who may be called the "free practical mind," that is to say, the man who is interested in political questions but who refuses to attach himself to a party or government so obsequiously and so blindly that he gives up every right to criticize the goals or the methods adopted by them. One of our great problems arises from the difficulty intellectuals have in preserving their dignity and integrity as citizens and human beings while they work for the government. This is one of the many profound issues raised by the Oppenheimer case.

Having been kicked out of the government, having been prevented from riding on campaign trains, intellectuals are not doomed to remote scholarship, to joining only the American Association of University Professors, and to convincing "their fellow citizens of the responsibility and seriousness of their calling." This is much too abject a surrender. It implies that the free intellectual's social influence is a thing of the past, something which has been eliminated by the "vast impersonal forces" of history.

With this I cannot agree. In my opinion this dubious argument closes every avenue by which the intellectual can carry out his traditional cultural functions. True, the free practical intellectual who tries to familiarize himself with the facts of social life, to defend a set of values, and to advance plausible solutions to social problems, runs the risk of dilettantism. But so does any human being in an effort to solve his personal problems. And why speak so disparagingly of "the production of bright ideas for essentially practical purposes masking as intellectual activity"? Why speak as though there were a contradiction between producing ideas for practical purposes and engaging in intellectual activity? This is a conclusion which can be drawn only by those who accept the dichotomy between the yogi and the commissar, the metaphysician and the intellectual goon, as an exhaustive division of the life of the mind. But surely somewhere between the metaphysical journals and the gossip columns there is a place where an intellectual can still perform his traditional social functions — if he has ideas.

This conclusion does not force us to minimize the importance of pure scholarship. But if we are thinking of the intellectual as an effective force in politics, we must acknowledge that pure scholarship, for all of its importance, is hardly the medium through which intellectuals have usually made their practical impact on the political world. We can pursue scholarship in a mighty fortress defended by the American Civil Liberties Union, but this of itself won't win us the influence of an Erasmus or a Mill. We must regain those historic jobs of which we have been robbed. We can still be the spiritual custodians of what is good in our tradition and the implacable critics of what is bad. The tasks of the practical intellectual continue to be what they always have been: to pursue the truth, to expose sham and injustice, to seek ways of avoiding the destruction of the world, to help make it as happy and as sane as it can be. If such intellectuals are spurned by governments, by parties, by the public, or accepted only on impossible terms, they must go their own way and they must protest. But they cannot protest effectively unless they have something to say, and they cannot say anything worth hearing unless they have ideas. Therefore, let some practical intellectual produce the twentieth-century counterpart of Mill's essay *On Liberty*, for example, and he will prove beyond doubt that the intellectual is not obsolete.

Fortunately there are signs of a new era in philosophy. I hope they are reliable. For if some analytic philosophers will apply their methods to social and political ideas, they will do a great deal to ward off the attacks on English and American philosophy which are now so common among those who fail to understand that the days of sentimental encyclopedism are over. If philosophers contribute to the clarification of some of the most serious problems of men and then try to deal with them, they may help those who must decide practical questions. Those who want more than this from philosophers reveal their own weakness, not that of philosophy. For the ultimate decision of what to do is to be made by each man for himself, and those who seek catechisms, confessors, and commissars should look elsewhere.

2 ·

English Philosophy at Midcentury:
An American's Impressions

To a visiting American one of the most striking things about English philosophy today is the complete triumph of the analytic movement associated with the names of G. E. Moore, Bertrand Russell, and the late Ludwig Wittgenstein. Of course, as we shall see, profound differences within this movement make it extremely difficult to present one doctrinal platform to which these great philosophers and their followers would subscribe, but there are a number of common traits of significance which are illustrated in their writings and teachings. One of the first things to notice is how hostile to speculative metaphysics English philosophers have become, and how often they insist that philosophy as they conceive it is not a rival of ordinary language or science, but rather an activity intended to clarify both. We can hardly fail to observe how little concerned they are with advancing a moral philosophy in the sense of a guide to life, and how intensely preoccupied they are with finding out what we mean by or how we use the words 'good', 'bad', 'right', and 'wrong'. And having ventured this far in generalizing, we may observe how analytic philosophy in its later or positivistic phase has become absorbed with language; how it treats some traditional problems as the

products of linguistic confusion and how it has drastically revised the formulation of others.

Preoccupation with language was at one stage mainly a matter of formulating a so-called criterion of meaning. Since so
much talk was to be prohibited as meaningless by positivistic
standards, a criterion had to be devised which would allow
a sharp separation of the meaningful from the meaningless.
And since what was of major interest was something called
scientific meaning, it had to be made perfectly clear that much
of traditional metaphysics might evoke images or stimulate
action and still be scientifically meaningless. In order to placate
those who insisted on calling language meaningful even when
it did not satisfy what looked like the clear-cut requirements
of the theory of meaning a new category was invented, that
of emotive meaning. Into this category, poetry, metaphysics,
theology, and sometimes ethics were conveniently dumped.

The scientific and the emotive became the two great categories of language, and within the scientific another distinction was made between statements of mathematics and logic
on the one hand, and statements of empirical science on the
other. Statements of the first kind were said to be true by
virtue of the meanings of their terms, and not on the basis of
experiment or observation of the world; while statements of
the second kind were confirmable only by experiment and
observation. This distinction between analytic and synthetic
statements, as they were called respectively, together with that
between emotive and scientific language, became the two
great principles of positivistic analysis. 'Is it meaningful?' was
the first question to ask about any statement; if so, is it cognitive or emotive? And if cognitive, is it analytic or synthetic?

The present period of analytic philosophy has still not re-covered from the military charm of this method, and many philosophers still bark out these questions as if they were per-fectly clear. But there are others who have come to have seri-ous doubts about the extant versions of the positivistic cri-terion of meaning, and still others who question the clarity of the distinction between analytic and synthetic statements. The result is a way of doing philosophy which cannot be easily summarized in formulae. In my opinion this is desirable, pro-vided it does not result in a complete deterioration of the intel-lectual processes. After every dogmatic period of philosophy there comes a period of withdrawal and hesitation. The rational mood often gives way to the mystical, and philosophers are un-willing to say anything definite for fear of distorting the situa-tion or of misleading others. In such periods it is hard to dis-tinguish the genius from the quack, for ironically enough the quack flourishes in the protective mist created by the genius. Philosophy ceases to be a matter which others can check, but rather a matter of flair and smelling things out; a literary atti-tude dominates and the way of putting things becomes ex-tremely important.

My impression is that English philosophy is just emerging from such a misty period. There now seems to be a lively interest in saying things, in publishing books which others can examine carefully, and a certain amount of boredom with phi-losophy conceived as gesture. While it is difficult to discern any new catechism as arresting as that of earlier positivism, one thing is certain: English philosophy is not likely to return to anything like the metaphysical and epistemological specu-lation which preceded the emergence of analytic philosophy at the turn of the century. Responsible and careful linguistic analysis is here to stay, for a while at any rate.

To visiting Americans the most striking evidence of the academic triumph of linguistic philosophy is the conversion of Oxford. The university we had always regarded as the last haven of idealism, Platonism, Aristotelianism, and moral piety, is now a philosophical boom town where linguistic analysis is all the rage. Cambridge, of course, is the university of Moore, Russell, and Wittgenstein, and has long been known to us as an analytic and positivistic center, but now Oxford out-Cambridges Cambridge; it has switched to a victorious cause in philosophy.

In America we are experiencing a similar conversion, but a vast country is not easily conquered by new movements; old American philosophies, like certain American soldiers, never die — they do not even fade away. We have not yet come to the point where linguistic philosophy has attained the respectability it has in England, but we have come far in that direction. Almost all our able young philosophers have been influenced by some form of analytic philosophy. So much so that more traditional American professors are willing to sacrifice something they dismiss as cleverness and ingenuity for something else called vision, when they choose their successors. The partisans of traditional metaphysics and moral philosophy yearn for a bright young philosopher-prince who will come to slay all the positivistic dragons and restore philosophy to its ancient dignity and solemnity. I must confess that I have not met this attitude in England, but I am sure it must exist, and that there are many traditionalists who are patiently awaiting the day when the analytic movement will have spent itself.

Precisely because of the triumph of analytic philosophy, it is no longer possible to speak of it as a single undifferentiated movement; sects and varieties have appeared with the advance of the century. Even the superficial historian is likely to distinguish at least three strains and each of them will probably be identified with one of the three philosophers I have mentioned. Russell is the legendary leader of those who apply the techniques of mathematical logic to the problems of philosophy. No matter how often he repeats words that resemble Marx's '*Je ne suis pas Marxiste*', he is the hero of those who build new, artificial languages for the solution of ancient and modern puzzles. G. E. Moore will always be the patron saint of those who respect ordinary language and who are anxious to examine it in an effort to produce clear synonyms for key philosophical expressions. Wittgenstein abandoned both programmes for something which only the most devoted of his disciples are supposed to understand,* but which has been described as "therapeutic positivism" — the effort to get at the roots of the insoluble problems of philosophy in a way that will make us aware of how we come to ask our strange questions and, ultimately, to free us from the need to ask them again.

I have been unable to detect any fourth strain which a historian is likely to add to this list, but I am struck by the fact that the Russellian wing is much less active in England than it is in America. Philosophical attitudes seem to be much more influenced by Moore and Wittgenstein. In the United States there is considerable interest in mathematical logic, both as an

---

* When this essay was written Wittgenstein's posthumous work had not yet begun to appear.

independent discipline to be pursued for its own sake, and as an instrument for the solution of philosophical problems. But in England there is comparatively little interest in pure logic, and this is probably connected with a lack of interest in it as a tool for philosophy, though it would be hard to say which is cause and which effect.

The attitude of the mathematical logician toward ordinary language is often one of contempt. He frequently believes, following Russell, that ordinary language is the source of confusion and paradox. He often maintains that philosophers are deceived by the grammar of ordinary language into outrageously fallacious arguments. For example, they begin by observing that there is no such thing as Pegasus and then they ask themselves what the word 'Pegasus' denotes, because they hold the view (dictated by grammatical theory) that every true statement must be about something. But since by hypothesis Pegasus does not exist, it is difficult to say that the statement, 'There is no such thing as Pegasus', is about Pegasus. Yet grammar must be appeased, and so they conjure up something immaterial, like *the idea of Pegasus* or *the possibility of Pegasus* or what-not, in a frantic effort to produce a denotation for the word 'Pegasus', and in this way a mysterious entity is invented, presumably because of the weaknesses inherent in the grammar of ordinary language.

Just such invention has been the stimulus of a good deal of counterinvention on the part of logicians, and in Russell's case it called forth his famous Theory of Descriptions, once called a paradigm of philosophy. The details of this theory need not detain us. It leads to the proposal that we translate a puzzle-producing statement like 'There is no such thing as Pegasus' with the help of mathematical logic, and it is held that once we get it into philosophically disinfected language, we shall no longer be tempted to invent anything as weird as the denotation of 'Pegasus'. 'Pegasus' is defined as 'the winged horse captured by Bellerophon', and 'There is no such thing as Pegasus' is then translated as 'It isn't true that Bellerophon captured one and only one winged horse'. In its new logically official formulation the statement does not contain the word 'Pegasus', and so the need for appeasing the grammarian in philosophically absurd ways has been removed. The moral of this example is obvious. We must reformulate the infected parts of our language (and they are many, it is held); we must build a system which will be free of these puzzle-producing and entity-breeding features. In some of his writings Russell has called the principle underlying this theory the supreme principle of philosophy — Occam's Razor, whose purpose is the elimination of all the queer entities born of the grammatical features of ordinary language and uncritical science.

Almost all analytic philosophers join with Russell in denouncing things as strange as the denotation of 'Pegasus'. And underlying this denunciation is the great bond between many analysts of ordinary language and mathematical logicians with a philosophical conscience. I think a similar principle motivated Wittgenstein's attack on the view that the meaning of a word (as opposed to its denotation) is some extralinguistic entity. It also explains Gilbert Ryle's hostility to the view that the mind is a ghostly inhabitant of a mechanical body. In effect, both of them urge us to reformulate our statements about *meanings* and *minds* in ways that are less misleading, less liable to suggest the existence of queer entities.

Where analytic philosophers usually differ is in their location of the source of the infection and hence in their views of the way to stop it. Those who follow Russell tend to blame the statements of ordinary language and accordingly advocate a policy of translating them into philosophically sanitary surroundings. Most English philosophers, however, join Moore in adopting a much more sympathetic attitude toward the habits of the man in the street. Any many argue, therefore, that ordinary language has no part in the difficulties which inspired Russell's theory of descriptions; they even hold that disembodied possibilities, meanings, and minds would never have been invented were it not for the linguistic confusions of Plato and Descartes. On this view, if only the habits of the man in the street had been seriously adopted, rather than the corrupt machinations of muddled philosophers, the elaborate constructions of the Russellians would never have been necessary. The result is a certain amount of hostility to the various devices introduced by Russell in accordance with Occam's Razor. The theory of descriptions has been attacked by younger philosophers; they have criticized phenomenalism, the philosophy which Russell and his followers adopt in order to dispense with the traditional Aristotelian doctrine of substance; they regard so-called *sense-data* as bogus philosophical pills which are worse than the disease they are supposed to cure.

It should be pointed out, therefore, that the hostility which these admirers of ordinary language feel toward the constructions of the logicians is not merely a matter of deploring the wasted energy involved in building new systems; it is also directed against the philosophical doctrines that have been smuggled into the artificial languages of some logicians. The one thing a hospital should not do is to spread disease, say the critics of logical reconstruction; and it must be admitted that many master-builders of supposedly disinfected languages have often forgotten or disregarded that maxim. For example, Frege, who was one of the greatest of all logicians and who is now being revived both in England and in America, has no qualms about postulating all kinds of queer entities. The queerest are called 'The True' and its mate 'The False'. Ironically enough, in America today this kind of talk is defended on so-called pragmatic grounds while the spirit of American pragmatism (with notable lapses on the part of William James and Charles Peirce) cries out against it. How it is justified by its admirers in England, I do not know.

What this shows, of course, is that proficiency in mathematical logic is no guarantee of philosophical insight. But then neither is proficiency in the use of the English language. I think it absurd to say that all translation into logical terminology has been helpful but I think it equally absurd to say that ordinary language is never responsible for philosophical confusion and error. And when ordinary language is responsible, philosophers do suggest alternative ways of talking which will avoid confusion, puzzlement, or the creation of bogus entities. To this extent all of philosophy involves linguistic reconstruction. What may divide some philosophers from others is their different conceptions of reconstruction, because some are more friendly toward mathematical logic than others.

In spite of the great achievements of Whitehead and Russell in the field of logical analysis, English philosophy, even of the analytic variety, is dominated by a suspicion of logical jargon.

But this can hardly be justified by mere hostility to artificial terminology, because contemporary English philosophy is filled with technically used terms, like 'meaning', 'rules', and 'category-mistake', to mention only the favorites. Philosophy, like every discipline which uses terms not ordinarily used by the man in the street, has a jargon. What counts is whether the jargon contributes to illumination and clarification, and unfortunately we have no litmus-test for that.

American philosophers are more interested in science both as an object of philosophical analysis and as an aid to philosophy. Many of them freely use the parts of logic they find clear, and some even think that empirical psychology is relevant to philosophical problems connected with meaning. On the other hand, English philosophers are playing their important and traditional role of warning against the dangers of scholastic verbiage masquerading as science and philosophy. It is pleasant to report that this is carried on with great zest and vigilance at Oxford, where I spent most of my visit to England, and it is encouraging to know that, in England, free and critical examination of the remote questions of philosophy still goes on, especially in times like these.

3 ·

Meta-meta-metaphysics:
A Later Look at English Philosophy

W E have already seen that one of the most conspicuous
features of analytic philosophy in the twentieth century is its
extraordinary preoccupation with its own aims and methods.
And no one can deny that this has been valuable. When one
is clearer about what one is trying to do, one has a better
chance of doing it. However, there is a point in this process
of self-examination at which one begins to worry about when
the prologue will cease and whether the play itself will ever
begin. I have this feeling about a recent collection of essays *
by eleven Oxford dons and one from the University of Melbourne. It begins with a lucid essay jointly written by H. P.
Grice, D. F. Pears, and P. F. Strawson, in which various conceptions of metaphysics are outlined, but then, instead of
producing essays *in* metaphysical thinking as they conceive it,
too many of the other authors just go on writing more *about*
metaphysical systems, *about* metaphysical arguments, *about*
the different kinds of criticisms which have been and may be

---

* *The Nature of Metaphysics*, edited by D. F. Pears. Contributors:
H. P. Grice, D. F. Pears, P. F. Strawson, S. N. Hampshire, B. A. O. Williams, Gerd Buchdahl, P. L. Gardiner, Iris Murdoch, G. J. Warnock, Gilbert Ryle, Mary Warnock, A. M. Quinton. The essays originated as talks
in the Third Programme of the B.B.C. (Published by Macmillan, London,
and St. Martin's Press, New York, 1957.)

leveled against metaphysics. The result is on the whole very disappointing, especially to a sympathetic student of recent Oxford philosophy. To listeners to the Third Programme who are philosophers many of the talks upon which these essays are based must have seemed superficial, to those who are not they must have seemed incomprehensible. With few exceptions the essays introduce people to a difficult discipline in the worst possible way, by describing it rather than by doing it for them or with them. Ironically such essays sin against a salutary principle of present-day Oxford: that philosophy should be done with a minimum of programmatic talk; and by contrast those essays in which metaphysics is discussed in relation to more concrete subjects — "Science and Metaphysics" by Gerd Buchdahl, "Metaphysics and History" by P. L. Gardiner, and "Metaphysics and Ethics" by Iris Murdoch — are like food to a man who has been studying menus for days. Not only menus which tell him what may be eaten, but also diets which tell him what may not be eaten; and, in the case of G. J. Warnock's essay, "Criticisms of Metaphysics," a manual on how to prepare menus, a survey of criticisms of metaphysicians whose main conclusion, so far as I can see, is the plausible view that we must not criticize them without reading them.

I have another impression of this tendency to discuss metaphysics in programmatic terms. I suspect that most of the authors have never done metaphysics on the scale conceived in this volume. Some of them have been educated under the influence of the antimetaphysical positivism of Professor Ayer's *Language, Truth and Logic*; others have been affected by Kantian doubts about metaphysics; still others may once have identified themselves with Wittgenstein's therapeutic approach to metaphysical illness. But now that they have re-discovered systematic metaphysics, they do not return with the evangelical passion of ex-sinners prepared to die for God, freedom, and immortality. They come back in a sober and cautious way, so that one feels that the most they want to say for metaphysics is "Well, the old thing isn't so bad after all, and maybe something can be done for it." But this approach will neither revive metaphysics nor give a clear idea of what it is. Most of the contributors keep assuring us that the task of metaphysics is grandiose "conceptual revision," that the metaphysician par excellence is not content with minor altera-tions in the map of thought, but that "with more or less of boldness, ingenuity and imagination, he re-draws the whole map" (p. 22). And yet when one thinks of what Oxford lin-guistic philosophers have been doing in the last few years, one becomes aware of a gulf between the aims of Oxford metaphysics and its achievements.

Having said this, I am embarrassed by my own situation as a reviewer, for if the authors' thoughts are removed from metaphysics, mine must be twice-removed. If they are *meta*-metaphysicians, I must perforce be a *meta-meta*-metaphysi-cian, since I shall try to show that some of their descriptions of metaphysics are vague or ambiguous and that the total effect of the volume is to present a blurred picture of the metaphysical animal. Because I cannot discuss the essays indi-vidually I shall confine myself to a few important themes run-ning through the volume.

In an age which is so hostile to metaphysics and so im-pressed by the achievements of science and mathematical logic, it is very important to show clearly how it is related to these other disciplines. And while several contributors try to distinguish the purpose, the subject matter, and the methods of metaphysics from those of natural science and everyday thinking, the abstractness of most of these discussions, the failure to *do* metaphysics seriously, leaves the relation between it and other subjects in an unclear state. Let me begin by illustrating this by reference to the introductory essay.

At one point the authors mention the view that metaphysics is "a supremely general study which is somehow presupposed by the special sciences" (p. 2) and remark that while Bradley believed that metaphysics was general, he would have ridiculed the idea that it was concerned to get at the presuppositions of science. But what about this word "presupposition" which is so central here? We are told that the relation between the presuppositions of science and its statements is not the relation between axioms and theorems, or that of the most general to the less general laws of nature. And we are left to guess that metaphysical presuppositions are not consequences which follow from scientific statements or from statements of ordinary life (though a later essay by B. A. O. Williams leads us to think otherwise). The best that the writers of the introduction can do here is to report what Kant said, namely, that metaphysical presuppositions state the conditions under which alone scientific knowledge of nature is possible, that they embody the conditions of the possibility of science and of ordinary everyday knowledge. And then the writers add: "Whatever the shortcomings of Kant's doctrine, it at least gives a clear meaning to saying that metaphysics is concerned with the presuppositions of science" (p. 7). But I do not find this clear and I doubt that persons to whom this essay is primarily addressed will find it clear. Most of us think of science as a human activity and believe it would not exist if there were no human beings. Are we to conclude that the existence of human beings "observing and acting from a particular position in time and space," to use Mr. Hampshire's words (p. 31), is a metaphysical presupposition of science? We normally think of the existence of human beings as a matter to be settled by common sense or by elementary biology. How, in that case, can we accept a formulation which appears to make the statement that there are human beings a metaphysical statement too, when metaphysics is sharply distinguished from science? One might at this point say, as Mary Warnock does in the "Final Discussion," that "Absolutely any statement could be metaphysical" (p. 153) but I do not think that this goes very well with the view that metaphysical statements are those which embody the conditions of the possibility of science, unless we are willing to say what seems absurd, namely, that any statement might formulate such a condition.

A principal theme of the volume is that metaphysics is "an attempt to re-order or re-organize the set of ideas with which we think about the world." But, as Grice, Pears, and Strawson indicate, scientists also engage in such activity and therefore metaphysical revision must be distinguished from departmental scientific revisions. How is this distinction to be made? By pointing out, they say, that "among the concepts [the metaphysician] manipulates are always some — like those of knowledge, existence, identity, reality — which, as Aristotle said, are common to all the departmental studies" (pp. 21–22). But mathematical logic also confines itself to using terms common to all the disciplines, terms like 'every', 'exists', 'is', 'not', 'is identical with'. How, then, shall we distinguish metaphysical revision from logical revision? Many contemporary Oxford philosophers have been indifferent to, indeed hostile to, mathematical logic, but shouldn't they try to show, in the light of this striking similarity, how mathematical logic is related to metaphysics as they conceive it?

The influence of modern logic on one of the contributors, Stuart Hampshire, may be seen when he says that "In the last thirty years philosophers have seen more clearly why the conditions of application of 'certain' and 'uncertain', as of 'same', 'true', 'exist', must vary with every type of term, and with every type of statement, with which they are combined" (p. 30). But if one of the things Hampshire has in mind is Russell's theory of types, it is important to remember that there are logical systems which dispense with it. This might have bearing on whether there is such a thing as a supremely general metaphysics. For if Hampshire were right about the necessary equivocality of metaphysical terms, if each of them assumed a different meaning in each of the special disciplines, each special discipline would require its own metaphysical map. For example, the metaphysician of natural science would, on Hampshire's view, discover a use of 'exists' in physics different from that discovered by the metaphysician of mathematics. And similarly for the other expressions. But then which of these different metaphysicians "would provide us with the outlines of the map of human knowledge" in Hampshire's words (p. 31)? Isn't he forced to say that every map is, as it were, a map of one country and that it is impossible to draw an unambiguous map of the whole cognitive world? In any case meta-metaphysical a priorism is not likely to get us very far here. What we should do is to make the map or maps and not confine ourselves to the theory of intellectual cartography. And if we try to do this, I suspect that we shall do it badly if we do not take into account the closely related work of the symbolic logicians.

I now turn to another persistent theme of this volume, namely, that the *method* of metaphysics is radically different from that used in natural science. It is said that "the methods of science, the tests for acceptability of scientific laws, remain quite different from the methods of metaphysics and the test for acceptability of metaphysical principles" (pp. 6–7), but one finds it hard to discover a clear positive view of metaphysical method which is consistently maintained throughout the volume. Williams says that *inductive* argument is not appropriate in metaphysics because metaphysical conclusions are necessarily true, even though he also says that a "prime characteristic of metaphysical argument [is] its use to establish propositions of existence or non-existence" (p. 55). On the other hand, Professor Ryle implies in the "Final Discussion" that *deductive* argument is inappropriate in metaphysics because "Hume and Kant exposed the fallaciousness of all arguments from purely conceptual considerations to positive existence-conclusions and none of our present team has, I gather, any inclination to rehabilitate them. Ontologizing is out" (p. 149). Moreover, Hampshire insists that deductive metaphysics has "been killed stone dead." So now we may ask whether Williams, who believes that we can deductively establish existential statements in metaphysics, is a member of the team. He illustrates metaphysical argument by deductive reasoning which moves from "the logical possibility of misrecognition, the existence of such a concept" (p. 56) to the conclusion that there are such things as visual experiences. There is no fear of ontologizing here and no fear of using "arguments from purely conceptual considerations to positive existence-conclusions."

Williams adds that the purpose of the argument which concludes that we have visual experiences both when we recognize tables and when we misrecognize them, "is not just to deduce a conclusion from the facts. It is rather to show that the account of those facts, when we reflect on them, has a hole in it, a hole which is exactly fitted by the metaphysician's special concept" (p. 57). And then Williams says that "The greatness of a metaphysician . . . is to be determined by three considerations: how arbitrary his special concepts are, how much they explain, and how much they distort our ordinary thinking" (p. 57). But how different are these methodological considerations from those which determine the greatness of natural scientists? After all, scientific concepts like that of the neutrino are also intended to explain and to fill a hole. And what is the difference between the psychological genius — a natural scientist — and Williams' metaphysical genius whose "concepts will explain a lot, by revealing important analogies between kinds of experience and thought which superficially seem widely different" (p. 57)? So far as I can see, the only way in which Williams can prevent his methodological description of the metaphysician from fitting the natural scientist is by insisting that the metaphysician, by contrast to the natural scientist, *deduces* existential conclusions from "purely conceptual" assumptions. But when he does this he splits the

Oxford "team" wide apart on the method of metaphysics, as we have seen, and he leaves the reader in bewilderment and confusion. At this point the reader who is not a professional philosopher and who is at the mercy of his disputing guides may justly complain that he has been abandoned in the metaphysical jungle without even a way of identifying the animals.

Some of our authors may have thought about such difficulties, but there is little sign of such thought in this volume. In part, perhaps, because of the need to simplify for purposes of popular exposition, in part because of too great an anxiety about making cut and dried distinctions between the various disciplines, one of the dreariest legacies of Aristotle. This passion for distinguishing subjects in an excessively neat way is best left by serious philosophers to those who are responsible for making up university budgets and assigning living quarters. Because it avoids this kind of scholasticism, the essay "Science and Metaphysics" by Gerd Buchdahl, the Melbourne contributor, is one of the most refreshing essays in the volume. Buchdahl does not try to define metaphysics by reference to the concepts it manipulates, he does not talk about conceptual revision in the blue, he does not fall back on the hazy map-metaphor, he does not involve himself in talk about "presuppositions." What he does is to show how in the course of reflection on physics a number of assertions have been made by distinguished thinkers which, because they do not seem testable by reference to ordinary scientific methods, have a peculiar and puzzling status. In this connection his discussion of different reactions to atomic theory is most helpful.

On the one hand, Buchdahl says, we want to say that atoms

are the building blocks of the universe. On the other hand we must acknowledge that we only have indirect evidence of their existence, and this gives rise to a puzzle. Although in the latter half of the nineteenth century Maxwell, Boltzmann, J. J. Thomson, and others had supplied increasing evidence for the existence of atoms, both Ostwald and Mach remained agnostic on the point. After the work of Einstein, Perrin, Wilson, Millikan, and others, Ostwald yielded but Mach remained adamant. Ostwald felt that scientific evidence now warranted the statement that atoms exist, but Mach continued to grumble that he could not "accept the existence of atoms and other such dogma" (p. 67). Underlying Mach's attitude, according to Buchdahl, was the view that "nothing can count as real or existent except an element of sensation" (p. 67) and this assertion, Buchdahl points out, was not subject to tests customarily used in science itself because no developments in science would have been capable of changing Mach's views. Some philosophers might ask whether Mach's assertion served any acceptable purpose, and although Buchdahl does not take us as far as we should like to go in answering this question, he does say some interesting things about the arbitrary character of assertions like Mach's and also about their positive function in the history of science. He also says some suggestive things about some metaphysical disputes, as for example: "One may describe this as a mere dispute as to what to *say* about certain definite empirical situations. Only, we should remember that we are not in possession of any *rules* which would tell us what to say. And so insensibly we are driven to take our stand somewhere." This very shrewd remark leads us to see that there are forms of intellectual activity whose results may not be tested by easily formulable methods or rules, but which may nevertheless be connected with well-regulated types of intellectual activity in a complex way. It was in this spirit, Buchdahl says, that Wittgenstein remarked in the *Tractatus* that "Men had indeed an idea that there must be a 'law of least action' before they knew exactly how it ran."

In concluding I should like to repeat my impression that we are more likely to learn about the springs and possibilities of metaphysics from studies like Buchdahl's than we are by rehashing the works of traditional philosophers without attention to logic or to the special disciplines which convey an enormously important part of the knowledge metaphysics is supposed to map. For if metaphysics is a worth-while effort to redraw the map of knowledge in the twentieth century, it can only be advanced by those who have done some intellectual traveling, part of it in the sciences.

4 ·

Two Positivist Philosophers

I. Richard von Mises

By contrast to the philosophers discussed in the last essay, the late Professor Richard von Mises traveled quite extensively in the sciences. If anything, his work suffers from a tendency to exaggerate the scope of scientific method. When his book *Positivism* * first appeared in German in 1939, logical positivism was a comparatively young philosophy which Europeans had known ever since the appearance of Wittgenstein's oracular and brilliant *Tractatus Logico-Philosophicus* in 1921. It was still a modish philosophy in the 1930's when our young traveling fellows were carrying home the doctrine of the Vienna Circle, but time has rubbed off a bit of its bloom and blunted some of its thorns. The philosophy of science, sponsored by positivists when it was a philosophical pariah, is now an important philosophical discipline and symbolic logic, that natural child of mathematics and philosophy, has become the respectable concern of a distinguished journal and the full-time specialty of a galaxy of scholars. A good deal has happened since those days when it was worth a graduate student's academic life to be caught turning the pages of Carnap, Reichenbach, or Wittgenstein unless he was scrawling nasty remarks in the margins. Some of those students have survived to become professors of philosophy both here and in England,

* Harvard University Press, Cambridge, 1951.

and the result has undoubtedly been a general elevation of philosophical thinking and writing — an upward trend that is not without its own dreadful dips, but nevertheless an upward trend.

From the very beginning the movement was not monolithic in character. Differences of attitude have been evident within it for more than thirty years and for this reason we must realize that a book baldly entitled "Positivism" is not likely to be an introduction to a philosophy shared by all so-called positivists. A few historical observations may help to show why.

Wittgenstein's *Tractatus*, in which so many of the positivistic slogans were first set down, was not a conventional treatise or catechistic handbook, and many of its more literal-minded admirers were made somewhat uneasy by its strange metaphorical obscurity, its intellectual waywardness. The up-shot was a kind of organized house-cleaning movement (in which Wittgenstein himself appears to have taken no part), dominated by the shrewd suspicion that clarity should begin at home. The partisans of positivism without tears banded themselves into circles and congresses much as the Marxist intellectuals did in the 1930's, and they set themselves the task of advancing the cause. Their central theme was that philosophy wasn't just another discipline on a par with the sciences, having a subject matter of its own, but that it was rather concerned with the analysis of scientific language and method. And because so many continental positivists were themselves scientists and not philosophical "pros," the analysis of ordinary language (as opposed to science) was left to the English analysts under the leadership of G. E. Moore, who, as the late J. M. Keynes has told us, was admired and feared by the

Bloomsbury group, constantly terrorizing them with one question: "What *exactly* do you mean?" Bertrand Russell, on the other hand, for whom ordinary language has always been the "metaphysics of the stone age," became a prophet more honored in Vienna than in his own Cambridge, and symbolic logic was celebrated in Vienna as the primary instrument in the analysis of scientific language; indeed, for Rudolf Carnap philosophy was *nothing but* the logical analysis of science.

The years following the *Tractatus* were devoted to formulating, among other things, an airtight criterion for scientifically meaningful statements as opposed to hated metaphysical statements. How can a positivist clearly characterize those sentences that are respectably scientific in character? How can we devise appropriate conditions for membership in the charmed circle, conditions which will exclude everything we want to exclude and at the same time not exclude too much?

All through this period one sensed an undercurrent of disagreement within the club. Science was proving so difficult — so refractory. No sooner did one formulate a criterion for being scientifically meaningful than the scientists would make statements which didn't fit into the ready-made shoes. Surely one couldn't say that the scientists themselves (qua scientists) were not talking scientifically; and so what about these criteria which always seemed to include too much or too little, these shoes that never seemed to fit the growing feet of science? Strangely enough, there developed within the very movement that despised Moore's concern with ordinary language a tendency to raise objections to excessive formalism very much like those which Moore had been raising against Russell's logical terminology for years. While Moore protested that the ordinary man didn't mean what Russell meant by the word 'implies', antiformalistic positivists made similar complaints on behalf of the scientist: "But this is not what scientists do!" To this the formal logicians replied that they weren't interested in merely giving a play-by-play account of the methods of science as practiced, in being Boswells for scientific Johnsons; they were rather interested in reconstructing science rationally, in reformulating it more clearly, in producing an ideal language. But this, in turn, was so far removed from the views of the Wittgenstein of the 1930's and 1940's (who had abandoned the views of his *Tractatus*) that it seemed absurd to continue to think of positivism as a single philosophical movement. Wittgenstein had become more and more interested in ordinary language, more and more concerned with the pathology of philosophical confusion growing out of failure to appreciate the subtle differences in the behavior of different kinds of words.

Now Mises was a representative of the less formalistic wing of logical positivism but, of course, nothing like the later Wittgenstein in the manner of his departure from more conventional positivistic slogans. In many ways he reminds one of American students of John Dewey and G. H. Mead who have been attracted to positivism, of pragmatists who have been brought up to think of science as a dynamic process and hence distrustful of excessively formal approaches to the theory of knowledge and meaning. Like Comte, Mises defended a positivism which was large and loose-fitting, covering as it did almost all corners of intellectual activity. Unlike most popular expositors of logical positivism Mises was a man of great culture and learning — an aeronautical engineer, a famous applied mathematician, and, surprisingly enough, one of the world's great collectors of Rilke. Mises' positivism does have a certain solidity, richness, and three-dimensional quality because he addresses himself to "Big Questions" surrounding the social sciences, religion, poetry, art, ethics, and the law. On many of these questions Mises wrote with impressive learning and authority, especially on certain points in the philosophy of physics and on the relation between the natural and social sciences. But one gets a rather different impression of his reflections on poetry, art, and ethics, and of his views on fundamental questions of the theory of knowledge, where a fineness of grain is demanded of a philosopher and where thinness in this sense is absolutely necessary.

Positivists have always had some difficulty in explaining the relations between the statements of empirical science, those of logic, and those of poetry. The most typical solution of the problem led to the view that statements of empirical science were "about reality" and meaningful in the strictest sense but that statements of logic were not "about reality" because they were "true by convention." Poetry was a very difficult affair in which positivists weren't particularly interested and as a rule it was granted a sort of second-class citizenship in the republic of sentences — it was assigned "emotive meaning" and hence not required to be "about reality." Now Mises had, for a positivist, somewhat unorthodox views on both poetry and logic. These views were motivated by a laudable desire to avoid these sledge-hammer distinctions, but unfortunately his accomplishments were less laudable than his motives.

For example, it is misleading or false to say as he did without elaborate qualification that what the poet "reports" are "ex-

periences about vital relations between observable phenomena," and that "In areas of life that are not sufficiently ex-
plored by science, poetry expresses, by means of linguistic
forms which have been created for that special purpose, experiences that are present in the consciousness of the poets in
the form of moods, feelings, or inspirations, with the aim of
communicating these states of consciousness to the reader or
listener." One almost gets the impression from Mises' porten-
tous reference to "areas of life that are not sufficiently ex-
plored by science" that poetry is a kind of primitive attempt
at science, something that will pass away when we are able to
convey these "states of consciousness" more efficiently. Surely
the passage he cites from Rilke's *Malte Laurids Brigge*, beginning:

verses are not, as people imagine, simply feelings (those one has
early enough) — they are experiences. For the sake of a single
verse one must see many cities, men, and things; one must know
the animals; one must feel how the birds fly and know the gesture
with which the little flowers open up in the morning,

surely, this is not enough to demonstrate what Mises calls the
"empirical character of lyric poetry." For the lyric poet, unlike the biologist, is not concerned to produce something
whose success depends wholly on whether or not the birds *do*
fly or the little flowers *do* open up as described. Even in those
cases where the poet does wish to convey experiences of the
kind Rilke describes, there is a difference between his mode
of conveying them and the scientist's, and this difference is
something one is likely to ignore when one talks of the "empirical character of lyrical poetry" and the "empirical character of biology" in one breath.

· 41 ·

Mises' desire to assimilate so much to empirical science is also expressed in what he says about logic, where he adopts extremely heterodox views for a positivist, views which he does not hold consistently. Unlike some of his philosophical friends, Mises holds that logic is "the physics of all things." But he also says that physics says something about reality *and* that logic doesn't, and this looks very much like what the "school philosophers" (as Mises calls them with contempt) would rightly call an inconsistent triad.

In spite of reservations about it, I think Mises' *Positivism* is a welcome antidote to the "hip-two-three-four" variety of philosophy whose sergeants initiate the poor student first by shouting "Is it meaningful or metaphysical?", rapidly follow up with "Cognitive or emotive?", and then produce that philosophical haymaker: "Analytic or synthetic?" Mises' book is what might be expected of a civilized, philosophical scientist who justly deplored the amount of rubbish which had been written by obscurantists but who couldn't bring himself to support some of the more scholastic tendencies in positivism itself.

II. *A. J. Ayer*

It is fair to say that Professor Ayer's first book, *Language, Truth and Logic* (1936), was one of the most influential philosophical works of the last generation and that it has been responsible not only for illumination but also for a certain amount of positivist scholasticism. But his most recent work, *The Problem of Knowledge,** is something very different. It is the product of a great deal of serious, mature reflection and

* Penguin Books and Macmillan, London, and St. Martin's Press, New York, 1956.

represents a real effort to come to considered conclusions on some of the main problems of philosophy, conclusions which do not give the impression — as his earlier conclusions often do — of having been ground out in an oversimplified way on some sort of philosophical machine.

Like everything written by Ayer, *The Problem of Knowledge* is lucid, direct, and provocative. Very likely it will be widely used as a textbook, stimulate many critical articles in *Mind,* and become the subject of stormy meetings of the Aristotelian Society. Indeed, it may come to occupy a position in contemporary British philosophy comparable to that of Russell's *Problems of Philosophy* in 1912. Just as the latter epitomized the beliefs of an earlier English philosophical world stirred by the new ideas of Moore and Russell, so Ayer's book conveys, in very readable form, some central attitudes of the most recent phase of linguistic philosophy. And unlike many presentations of this point of view, it conveys its message without affectation, archness, or vulgarity, without mannered obscurity posing as ultimate clarity.

Ayer begins by saying that "the necessary and sufficient conditions for knowing that something is the case are first that what one is said to know be true, secondly that one be sure of it, and thirdly that one should have the right to be sure." In requiring the third condition, Ayer builds on a very influential paper by Professor J. L. Austin of Oxford, who insists on the titular character of knowledge, on the fact that knowing is not being in a state of mind that excels, on the same scale, the state of believing very firmly. Rather, the difference between knowing and believing very firmly consists in the fact that when we say we *know* we are claiming a *right* to believe firmly. No American philosopher will fail to see the extent to which this view of knowledge resembles that of William James, who once said that his famous paper "The Will to Believe" should have been called "The Right to Believe." Of course this similarity should not be exaggerated, because James went on to say some peculiar things about the way in which the right to believe could be justified, but it should be mentioned simply because of the indifference or hostility which English philosophers have always shown toward pragmatism. It is therefore interesting to observe Austin and Ayer converging with James on at least one point (as well as to observe the broad similarities between Dewey and Wittgenstein, both of whom opposed Cartesian dualism, Platonism, and the kind of formalism which focuses on the logical syntax of language rather than on its function and use).

Ayer introduces his definition of knowledge in order to consider the claims of the philosophical skeptic with whom he argues for the rest of the book. Ayer says that the skeptic need not reject this definition; on the contrary, he can exploit it. For if knowing that there is a cigarette case on this table implies having the right to be sure that there is, the skeptic will concentrate on the ways in which we defend our right to be sure of this and will maintain that they are all defective. In doing so he will be challenging our standards for establishing the legitimacy of the title to be sure. One may reply, as some philosophers do, that one is having an experience which is recorded in a so-called "sense-datum" statement, viz., 'It seems to me that I am seeing a cigarette case', and that the statement that there is a cigarette case on the table is validly derivable from this sense-datum statement. But Ayer says, on behalf of the skeptic and in opposition to the phenomenalist, that no number of such sense-datum statements would *logically* entail the conclusion that there is a cigarette case on the table. Therefore, if the skeptic insists that we must *deduce* the statement that there is a cigarette case on the table from the sense-datum statement, he is making a demand which we cannot satisfy because of the very way in which we use sentences which are taken as referring to physical objects. The skeptic's victory is therefore bloodless. "It is characteristic of what is meant by such a sentence as 'there is a cigarette case on this table' that my having just the experience that I am having is evidence for the truth of the statement which it expresses. The skeptic is indeed right in his insistence that there is a gap to be overcome, in the sense that my having just this experience is consistent with the statement's being false; and he is right in denying that a statement of this kind can be reduced to a set of statements about one's sense-experiences, that is, to a set of statements about the way that things would seem. He is wrong only in inferring from this that we cannot have any justification for it."

Now this is typical of the kind of argument which is offered at crucial points in this book. Our knowledge of the past and our knowledge of other minds have been the other traditional objects of skeptical doubts, and Ayer deals with these doubts in similar ways. I do not have the space in which to report Ayer's many subtle discussions of problems in this area because I should like to comment on his general method of answering the skeptic.

There is, of course, a difference between a deductive argument for a conclusion and one which appeals to experience. But from this it does not follow that the philosophical defense of the legitimacy of deduction as such is fundamentally different from the philosophical defense of the practice of basing knowledge on experience. Confusion arises when some philosophers try to defend all of deduction by saying that its legitimacy depends on the fact that the meaning of the premises contains the meaning of the conclusion, because then it seems right to say in contrast that the meaning of 'It seems to me that I am seeing a cigarette case' does not contain the meaning of 'There is a cigarette case on the table'. We are given the misleading impression that *the reason why* we have the right to pass from the premise to the conclusion in the case of deduction is the fact that floating entities called meanings are related in certain ways when we deduce correctly, whereas a similar backing is not available when we move from a sense-datum statement to a statement about the existence of the cigarette case. But many contemporary philosophers are not likely to let so much rest on these floating meanings even if they should be willing to speak temporarily with more vulgar philosophers. They are likely to say that when we speak of these relations between the meanings of premise and conclusion in a deductive argument, we are saying in misleading picturesque language what had best be said by pointing out that the adequacy of deduction as such depends on how we use sentences which form the premises and conclusions of deductive arguments. And if we take this line, what more can we say than this: that in deduction we *use* sentences in such a way as to grant us the right to be sure of the conclusion if we are sure of the premise? But this is precisely the kind of answer that Ayer gives in defense of the general practice of basing our knowledge claims on experience.

In both cases we can do no more than appeal to the accepted code for the transmissibility of the right to be sure; we appeal to the accepted way of speaking. Trying to justify the code *as a whole* in any more profound way is like trying to lift ourselves by our own bootstraps. We cannot find an Archimedean point outside of the structure for judging or budging the structure itself. We may question or revise specific standards for earning the right to be sure, deductive or otherwise, but we find it hard to think of ourselves giving up deduction as such or giving up the practice of basing knowledge upon experience. We are tempted to think we can because we draw an analogy between a code that sets up standards for the right to be sure and a moral code. In the latter case we feel that we can review the code that we *do* use in order to find a better one. But it is one thing to revise moral codes in specific ways and another to justify moral judgment as such, i.e., to justify the general practice of saying what ought or ought not to be done by reference to some standard or other. The request for such a justification of moral judgment lacks meaning, as do the analogous requests for justifications of deduction and basing our knowledge on experience. We engage in certain regulated practices like deduction, moral judgment, and scientific theorizing, whose patterns the philosophically minded person tries to discover and to express in principles. The deductive logicians have been the most successful in presenting such principles but even they cannot produce a mechanical criterion which will allow us to test all our principles of inference. When our practices change we may recast our rules but we are always moving back and forth from practice to rule and there is no rock which can serve as a fulcrum on which the claims of each can be weighed in some absolutely decisive way. The notion that there is such a rock is one of the great chimeras of western thought. To have done something to eliminate this chimera is one of the great merits of Professor Ayer's book and of the philosophical tendency which he so brilliantly represents.

5 ·

Harvard's Philosophical Heritage

A PHILOSOPHICAL movement that affected Vienna, Cambridge, and Oxford so seriously could hardly have left Harvard untouched, and for this reason it is easy to imagine questions being asked by those whose conception of the subject had been formed in an earlier generation: "What has happened to philosophy at Harvard? Where is the Alpine splendor of Royce's absolute idealism, the playful practicality of James, and the literate Latin naturalism of Santayana? All melted away! And what do we see now but a wasteland of linguistic analysis, a verbalistic desert, a dusty retreat without even a Whitehead in evidence to blow the metaphysical bugle or to cover the stark logistics with clouds of wisdom?"

This might be the extreme reaction of a hostile, nostalgic critic of almost all of contemporary American philosophy. And although the invitation to write this article limits me to a description of philosophy at Harvard, what I have to say in reply holds for a considerable part of the American philosophical scene.

No discussion of Harvard philosophy can begin without a bow to those giants of the old days, Royce, James, and Santayana. And not merely a pious ceremonial bow, but one which sincerely celebrates their profound effect on the development of American philosophy in the twentieth century.

· 49 ·

Though this gesture may seem excessively ironical to those who see contemporary Anglo-American philosophy as depressingly different from philosophy in the Gay Nineties, it is a mistake to suppose that American philosophers have completely abandoned the traditional interests and humane concerns of Royce, James, and Santayana. Some American philosophers are interested in the problems of philosophical theology; in the problems posed by the arts, politics, morality, education; in the history of philosophy. And if they do not regularly issue large volumes reporting their "discoveries," this is the result of a great change in the subject which was promoted by James, Royce, and Santayana themselves in their deeper moments, a change which has not only radically altered the interests of many philosophers but which has even forced the traditionalists to set forth their views in a more guarded, less flamboyant way.

From a literary point of view this change has been reflected in the fact that the article or essay has come to be a very important means of scholarly communication, much as it is in science and mathematics. This has happened partly because of the need to pursue individual points meticulously and to submit them quickly to the scrutiny of one's professional colleagues, and partly because of a widespread conviction that philosophical reflection cannot always issue in a swollen, two-volume system which relates everything in the universe to everything else. This deflationary feature of contemporary philosophy is most striking in Great Britain and in the United States, where published collections of articles by many hands are far more common than they were fifty years ago. It represents a far cry from Royce, who, when he was once asked to write an article for a magazine, replied that he could not comply because he was "doing his thinking in book lengths." Since Royce's day the growth of rigor and the need for intellectual cooperation has affected the style of philosophy in a manner comparable to that in which it has affected the style of science, of history, and even of literary studies.

In the natural sciences and mathematics it is almost indecent to publish one's results in a book, and we are all aware of the scorn for Toynbee's massive productions which prevails among tough, monographic historians. And yet in spite of this universally acknowledged trend toward specialization in our time, philosophers are criticized for turning their attention to highly specialized questions. One is almost led to think that the self-doubts of the rest of the scholarly world in this regard have been concentrated and outwardly directed in resentment at the philosopher for not keeping up a practice which everyone else has been compelled to abandon. No doubt there is some historical justification for this attitude, because philosophy has been the traditional custodian of the big questions. But a big question need not call for a big or pompous answer, as the dialogues of Plato show.

The critic who nostalgically recalls the Harvard Philosophy Department at the turn of the century is too often affected by a need to clothe the past in a warm mist that may obscure the important features of the philosophical accomplishments of James, Royce, and Santayana. He understandably thinks of them as they lived in their lecture halls or in their more popular works, unconstrained by the need for professional rigor or by the demands of the scholarly journal. And therefore he may not remember the labored pages in which Royce distinguished between the internal meaning and the external meaning of an idea; nor is he likely to recall those writings of James in which he struggled to expound his radical empiricism or to answer critics who asked him to say which of the thirteen varieties of pragmatism was his own. Because of his interest in the more popular aspects of their work, the layman may miss just those qualities which show how James and Royce continue to affect contemporary philosophy. James may have been very stimulating when he talked to teachers, and Santayana may have been brilliant in some of his reflections on the United States, but both of them aspired to greatness in their technical work, and it is this which will live in the history of American philosophy. In the same way David Hume is not famous for his best-selling and now unread *History of England* but rather for his *Treatise of Human Nature*, which, as he said, "fell still-born from the press," and Kant is perpetually remembered for his work on space and not for his work on perpetual peace.

In short, the great Harvard philosophers were not Sunday supplement scholars; they were primarily technical thinkers working on problems that baffled their predecessors from Plato to Hegel. In their effort to solve them or reconceive them, they laid the foundation for at least fifty years of vigorous, intensive philosophical investigation; and if philosophy in America is different from what it was at the turn of the century, it is different not because it has departed from the true spirit of the Harvard greats but because it has taken this spirit seriously. It has banked the gold of the golden age and left the gilt to others.

A contemporary British philosopher has said that one of the most important changes in the last half century of Anglo-American philosophy is what he calls the decline of the pontiff. But what is ironical about the "depontification" of philosophy in America is the fact that here it was initiated by the pontiffs themselves. This was strikingly true of Royce, the most magisterial of all the philosophers of the golden age, the most plush and world-encompassing of its pundits. For Royce was more than a metaphysical soothsayer, more than a philosopher of religion and of loyalty to loyalty: he was also a logician and a philosopher of science. He was one of the first American teachers of philosophy to recognize the importance of research in symbolic logic and to encourage its study both for its own intrinsic intellectual importance and as a tool. Some of his pupils, like C. I. Lewis and H. M. Sheffer, became distinguished Harvard contributors to this subject and founders of one of the most influential centers of logic in the twentieth century. One of the main effects of such logical study has been the encouragement of exactness and precision in philosophy. Today's philosopher is far less glib about saying "It follows" than his predecessors were a half-century ago. His "therefore"'s are scrutinized with as much care as those of mathematicians are, and for this reason he finds it much harder to pass off vast systems of deductive metaphysics on his wary colleagues.

The irony is that on the day that he announced his first course in modern logic, Royce initiated a chain of events which makes it virtually impossible for any American philosopher to publish as rambling a piece of argument as Royce's *World and the Individual*. As far back as the first decade of this century, his pupil Ralph Barton Perry was deflating the pretensions of idealistic metaphysics, its vagueness, and its fallacies with the help of logical techniques that Royce had introduced to the Harvard curriculum. Later Harvard philosophers turned more highly developed logical instruments on the realism of Perry and his friends, and very soon most American philosophers were made even more conscious of the fact that clarity begins at home. A whole generation of American philosophers came to worry about the nature and method of their subject, partly under the influence of modern logic and partly under the influence of another tendency which is deeply rooted in the Harvard tradition: pragmatism.

Harvard pragmatism grew out of patient reflection on the procedures of the natural sciences. Its originator was Charles S. Peirce, who not only encouraged Royce in his logical interests, but who first formulated the pragmatism which William James popularized and applied to subjects beyond the laboratory. Unfortunately for an earlier generation of Harvard students they were protected from direct contact with the eccentric genius of Peirce because he was thought not to measure up to the moral standards required of a professor in the nineteenth century. Later the Philosophy Department made some amends by publishing Peirce's *Collected Papers* posthumously, and they, together with the works of William James, contain the classic sources of Harvard's pragmatic tradition.

In their different ways Peirce and James encouraged Harvard philosophers to seek for the practical meaning of any statement. By doing so, they hoped, a great deal of idle and confusing language might be eliminated as meaningless because, as James and Peirce held, much philosophical talk cannot measure up to the pragmatic criterion of meaning and its appeal to empirical consequences. By using this criterion philosophers who think they disagree may come to see that they do not, and philosophers who think they are saying something may come to an even more disappointing conclusion. This was one of the most influential contributions to twentieth-century philosophy, and it combined with the doctrines of that great admirer of James and Peirce, John Dewey, with the highly self-conscious linguistic emphasis of logical positivism, and also with the philosophy of physics called operationalism, which was expounded so effectively by Professor Bridgman of the Harvard Physics Department and made so convincing by Einstein's redefinition of some of our basic scientific concepts.

Pragmatism, logical positivism, and operationalism all encouraged a tighter, more scientifically oriented, less monumental conception of philosophy. The new conception turned the attention of a generation of American graduate students away from speculative philosophy and more and more in the direction of analytic philosophy, to an interest in the clarification of the fundamental concepts of mathematics, science, and everyday life. And this generation, it will be admitted and even emphasized in lamentation by the opponents of analytic philosophy, now dominates Anglo-American thought. Its influence is felt in every important philosophical center in the English-speaking world.

Once again the development may be viewed as ironical, for Peirce and James did not foresee some of the consequences of their own pragmatic emphases. The more transcendental features of Peirce's metaphysics and his Spencerian ambition of constructing a system of all knowledge now seem hopelessly antiquated. James's Will to Believe, by means of which he hoped to salvage a number of traditional convictions, is inconsistent with the most commonly accepted versions of pragmatism and dangerously like what most men call wishful thinking. The combined forces of logic and pragmatism have undoubtedly brought about a drastic and irreversible alteration in the aims and standards of many American philosophers.

Although I believe that logic and pragmatism are two of the most powerful clauses in Harvard's philosophical legacy, I would not wish to give the impression that they are the only elements represented in the present department. In this article I do not speak for my colleagues, but as a historian of the philosophy of the recent past. Harvard philosophers, I hasten to point out lest I be accused of drawing a one-sided picture, speak for themselves in many different philosophical tongues. And this is surely in the Harvard tradition of diversity. James said "Damn the Absolute!" to Royce, Santayana was very critical of James, James described Santayana as "a representative of moribund Latinity," and in a later generation Hocking, Perry, Lewis, and Whitehead may well have said similar things about each other. But the historical trend of Anglo-American philosophy has been such as to call for a tougher, more dialectically self-conscious defense of these diverging doctrines since the intensification of the logical, pragmatic, and linguistic tendencies I have described. Because of this and despite all of their doctrinal differences Harvard philosophers share the conviction that the main instrument of philosophy is careful reasoning, and therefore those who deal seriously with theological problems resist the notion that they can be solved in a cheap and misleading way. They spurn the irrationalism and the double talk which can so often confuse the central questions of philosophy and theology, and for this reason they share a common platform with each other even when they cannot accept each other's conclusions. This is what separates them from the many irrational, obscurantist tendencies which have swept over the western world in its time of troubles.

Troubled times always dramatize the sheltered character of academic life, its preoccupation with questions that seem remote from the immediate demands of the society or the nation. And for this reason, I think, a philosophical tendency toward exactness which under happier circumstances could not but be regarded as salutary is suspected by those whose historical perspective should be longer than it is. We are living in an age which is so tormented by the problems of the cold war that some of us cannot help thinking that philosophers fiddle while the world freezes. The situation is made more complicated by the fact that in the past American philosophers were intensely occupied with practical and human questions.

In this vein a very shrewd observer of the American philosophical scene has recently said: "Philosophers in America have been less sheltered and cloistered than in Britain, in this century at least, partly because the universities themselves have been less protected from external pressures. Consequently the tone of American philosophy, in James, Dewey, and Whitehead, for instance, has tended to be more earnest, more consciously responsible, more prophetic, and also loud and emphatic enough to reach a large and attentive audience. Since Mill, and always excepting Russell, British philosophy has often seemed to be a quiet exchange between adepts in some learned discipline; the rougher note of the lay preacher is seldom heard and is always disliked. The result has sometimes been philosophy that is more careful and modest, but also more faint and genteel, more easily left on one side in the larger movement of ideas. Within the universities philosophy was significant principally as a training in exact argument, but it generally left beliefs, and even habits of thought, undisturbed." * He goes on to point out, however, that certain technical tendencies within philosophy itself have brought English and American philosophy closer together, and this alone may make us realize how different American philosophy is from what it was fifty years ago.

Even if one were to grant the premise of contemporary philosophy's most severe critics, as I do not, one could point to the disadvantages of trying by artificial means to channel it into an exclusively practical and hortatory direction. There is, for example, the undeniable connection between logical research and the construction of the computing machines which played so great a part in the development of the atomic bomb. But it would be grotesque to justify the study of technical philosophical questions in this spirit. To accept connection with the bomb as a measure of philosophical achievement is to betray the ideals which link us with Socrates, Mill, and Kant, to say nothing of James, Royce, and Santayana, and wrongly to imply that when philosophers cannot claim such "useful"

* Stuart Hampshire, "American and British Philosophy," *Encounter*, April 1957, pp. 78–79.

accomplishments, however indirectly, they have no reason for being.

On the other hand, I think it fair to criticize those philosophers who have so narrowly conceived their subject as to rule out *a priori* the pursuit of certain social, moral, esthetic, and political questions. The technical philosophical advances of the twentieth century should be admired by all who can understand them, but they certainly do not prove that the broad, humane preoccupations of a Royce, a James, and a Santayana are forever beyond the borders of philosophy. Indeed, certain recent tendencies suggest that another view is developing within the very tradition that has made so much of the logical study of language. Instead of maintaining, as some positivists have, that the only type of language worth studying philosophically is the language of science, a number of philosophers have come to believe there are many important uses of language which are not scientific and which may be studied with profit. This view is becoming more and more popular among the youngest generation of American philosophers and it may turn out to be the medium whereby philosophy will regain close contact with the humanistic tradition. For once it is recognized that the problem of knowledge is not the only problem in philosophy; once it is recognized that there are other modes of human activity which demand philosophical analysis and description, philosophy will cease to be equated with logic and the theory of perception. They will undoubtedly continue to be central subjects and no philosopher will risk the study of any other subject without a firm grasp of their fundamentals, but they will cease to constitute the essence of the discipline as they do for so many today.

Esthetics, the philosophy of education, the philosophy of history, and philosophy of religion, political philosophy, and jurisprudence will flourish as serious philosophical concerns and not be regarded as "soft subjects," fit only for lesser minds. When this happens on a larger scale in American philosophy, we shall have witnessed a new chapter in the development of the subject.

6 ·

A Plea for an Analytic Philosophy of History

As we have seen, there are many mansions of philosophy, but some are more luxuriously outfitted, larger, and better situated than others. High on a broad hilltop are the great homes of metaphysics, logic, epistemology, and ethics, while somewhere down below, huddled together on narrow streets, are the two-family dwellings of political philosophy and jurisprudence, the modern apartments of esthetics, and the boarding-houses for philosophers of the special sciences. The philosophy of history has never lived on the hill, not even in its most affluent days. Like esthetics and others among the poor relatives it has welcomed guests from the hill late in the day, often when they were weary and propelled by nothing more than the tourist's desire to see everything or, worse, the desire to *say* that they had seen everything.

The structure of the philosophical community is similar throughout the West and the plan presented is as accurate a description of the American tradition as it is of the European. Rightly or wrongly, no great western philosopher has ever been concerned exclusively or even primarily with the subsidiary disciplines. Hegel, for all of his preoccupation with history, was primarily a metaphysician of *process* and *becoming*. Even Russia, where the philosophy of history is held in such esteem, provides no significant exception if we are to judge by the way in which a metaphysics like dialectical materialism holds sway over the official conception of history. At most the Russians move the philosophy of history a little closer to the mandarin disciplines, rightly pointing out that elsewhere it is a vagrant, wandering aimlessly through the streets of philosophy and history. Hence its ambivalence and confusion. Like Rameau's nephew (and all poor relatives of the great) the philosophy of history spends half its time protesting its famous lineage and the other half offering its services as a sort of plumber's helper. One day it is the noble figure of universal history ("The subject of this course of lectures," said Hegel, "is the Philosophical History of the World"), on the next it offers to tutor the historian in the most elementary rules of method.

Partly because of the traditional tendency to think of the philosophy of history as one of the less fundamental disciplines, it was never studied systematically by any one of that group of distinguished thinkers who came upon the American scene after the Civil War and who inaugurated what is sometimes called the golden age of American philosophy: John Dewey, William James, Charles Peirce, Josiah Royce, and George Santayana. All of them were interested to some extent in the problems of the philosophy of history, but no one of them, with the possible exception of Santayana as we shall see presently, has left a large-scale contribution to it of either the speculative or epistemological kind. Unlike Hegel they avoided writing the "philosophical history of the world" and unlike Dilthey they did not try to write a "critique of historical reason." One might offer many explanations for this, and no doubt some of them would involve reference to more than intellectual considerations, but one important consideration is the fact that they thought of themselves as pioneers, destined to deal with the traditionally central problems of philosophy. In the revolutionary period men like Jefferson sought to build a political philosophy on foundations provided by Locke and his successors in England and France, while in the first half of the nineteenth century Emerson and his friends looked to the German romantics for a world-view that would support their moral and esthetic attitudes. But the philosophers of the end of the nineteenth century were at once more technical and less derivative in their thinking: they sought to devise more fundamental techniques for mining metaphysical, logical, and ethical gold. Royce, a Californian, dug the deepest shafts and emerged with his *World and the Individual* (1899); Santayana, an Americanized Spaniard, sought his philosophical fortune in the natural bases of morals and produced his *Life of Reason* (1905); while the easterners James, Dewey, and Peirce formed a pragmatic corporation which originated and developed America's most distinctive philosophy. For over a half-century these men, especially the pragmatists and the naturalists, dominated American philosophy, but their effect on the philosophy of history was felt mainly through the work of younger Americans with a more sustained interest in historical research.

How did the major philosophers of this period encourage interest in the philosophy of history even as they remained aloof and worked on other problems? For one thing, like so many who came to maturity in the nineteenth century, most of them shared a deep respect for the accomplishments of history and a sense of its centrality in the scheme of studies. This emerges most clearly in Royce's lectures *The Spirit of Modern Philosophy* (1892) and in his essay *Herbert Spencer* (1904). He pointed out sympathetically that the nineteenth century was more intensely interested in the historical aspect of things than in their permanent nature, that it was the century of the organic and humane sciences, that it added the motto "And yet it does grow" to Galileo's "And yet it does move." While Royce resented Herbert Spencer's crude evolutionary philosophy, he respected the great new science of Darwin and believed that the emergence of evolutionary biology had been blocked not so much by the theological idea of special creation or by post-Kantian idealism as by the predominance of mathematical and mechanical conceptions which prevented interest in the concept of growth.

Even Santayana, the disciple of Spinoza and the Greeks who scorned what he called Royce's idealistic theodicy, imagined himself under the spell of history. He tells us of his early absorption "in the historical spirit of the nineteenth century, and that splendid panorama of nations and religions, literatures and arts, which it unrolled before the imagination," and also of the influence Hegel exerted on him in spite of the "myth and sophistry" of Hegel's system. In his *Life of Reason*, which was subtitled "The Phases of Human Progress," Santayana tried to carry out something like the Hegelian program without dialectical tears and the result, in Santayana's genial metaphor, was a moral review of science, art, religion, and society in which the philosopher looked over western civilization and picked out his friends. *The Life of Reason* was, he said, an essay in retrospective politics, using the results of what, with Aristotle, he snobbishly called the servile science of history.

For all of his announced affection for the historical attitude of the nineteenth century we can see how little appreciation of it Santayana really had. He lacked all sense of its dynamic aspect; he lacked all interest in the growth of things. What he admired about the nineteenth century were its least distinctive qualities — its preparation of panoramas, of static pictures at an exhibition, rather than its effort to give life and meaning to those pictures. His interest in them, therefore, is essentially that of a museum visitor who appreciates the Rosetta Stone and the Elgin Marbles but who is wholly uninterested in their histories and their times.

If any philosopher was distinguished by his active interest in historical method it was John Dewey. An Hegelian in his youth, an admirer of Darwin, an educator, a psychologist, and a politically active intellectual in addition to being a great philosopher, Dewey took seriously the nineteenth-century concepts of growth and culture. It was Dewey who absorbed something from Hegel without missing his main point. Dewey's work in philosophy, along with the antiformalistic jurisprudence of Justice Holmes, the anticlassical economics of Thorstein Veblen, and the economically-oriented political science and history of Charles Beard and others, formed a coherent liberal American ideology in the first quarter of the twentieth century. These thinkers not only admired the splendid panoramas prepared by nineteenth-century economists, biologists, and historians, but tried to use them actively in an effort to reform the world and our beliefs about it. Like Santayana they rejected the rigidity of the Hegelian dialectic but in doing so imagined themselves pushing the historical attitude to its proper conclusion rather than abandoning it. What they rejected was the pretentiousness of speculative theories of history, but this did not mean that they sponsored the production of dreary chronicles or systems of "retrospective politics"; instead they sought documented syntheses like Beard's *Rise of American Civilization* (1927) and developed fruitful concepts for the investigation of American society like that of F. J. Turner's "Frontier." Some of them recognized that even this more modest enterprise required a selection of facts, and some of them came close to the extreme relativism implicit in Santayana's image of the philosophical historian picking out his friends. But this garden-party view of the historian's task meant pangs of conscience for those who were stern partisans of objectivity in social science. How to reconcile the unavoidable fact of selection with their liberal hatred of special pleading and the kind of history which deteriorated into distortion and propaganda under political domination? This became a central problem of the philosophy of history as it was discussed by a later generation of American philosophers and historians. It was, in a sense, a miniature replica of the problem which occupied the entire pragmatic tradition: how to emphasize the practical, experimental nature of knowledge without surrendering objectivity, without allowing its concepts of *usefulness* and *success* to be distorted and misinterpreted by those who make history a political weapon rather than a social tool?

From the point of view of philosophers the central problems of the philosophy of history were methodological or epistemological rather than speculative or metaphysical in character, a fact which reflects fashions and tensions within philosophy itself. In spite of the lingering influence of the classical tradition, American metaphysics suffered severe blows in the second quarter of the twentieth century just as it did in England. Chief among its assailants were the disciples of logical positivists and English analysts who attacked it sharply after pragmatism had softened it up. Methodology and logical analysis came to dominate the work of philosophers of history primarily interested in the nature of historical synthesis, the problem of historical explanation and causation, in the similarities and differences between history and the other disciplines, in the problem of historical imagination and the language of historical description.

The epistemological orientation of the American philosopher combines with the cautious, monographic bias of many American historians to diminish the likelihood of an American Spengler or Toynbee in the near future. The historian's distrust of undocumented speculation and the philosopher's suspicion of anything that might be labeled "meaningless" by positivistic or pragmatic standards have both contributed to this end. In recent years professional historians have not shown themselves devotees of historical speculation in the Herder-Vico-Hegel manner. During the 1930's, of course, Marxism was influential but often modified by those who pointed to Engels' admission that the ideological superstructure might sometimes influence the economic substructure. Since the decline of Marxism no single factor has caught the imagination of historians and philosophers, and the result has been a kind of unspectacular and sober pluralism, a tendency to say that *all* factors, economic, religious, intellectual, psychological, and political enter into historical explanation. This same caution has discouraged any serious interest in vast theories of historical change, which have never attracted Americans with anything like the force they have exerted on Europeans. Perhaps native resistance to them is due to "American exceptionalism," the belief that America is peculiarly set off from other civilizations. But then it might be a justifiable reaction to those samples of speculative history that have been prepared in America. The two extremes are represented by the theological optimism of George Bancroft and the thermodynamic pessimism of Brooks and Henry Adams.

Bancroft was one of the leading historians of the early nineteenth century and he expressed in the simplest and most direct terms a theological determinism which a later generation of tough-minded historians rejected with devastating finality. He believed in the necessity and actuality of human progress under divine auspices and defended it with all the rhetoric at his command. The young Charles Beard singled Bancroft out as Goliath and aimed at him on behalf of many social scientists and historians of his generation. Beard was a close student of two critical periods of American history, that surrounding the Constitutional Convention and that following the Civil War, and both seemed to upset Bancroft's Panglossian portrait of the universe. Like so many who have confronted optimistic theologians with the problem of evil, Beard in his *Economic Interpretation of the Constitution of the United States* (1913) defended the thesis that the Constitution was mainly a product of economic interest.

Well before Beard had launched his crusade a New England heretic, Brooks Adams, had published his *Law of Civilization and Decay* in 1896. He was not content to say merely that the doctrine of progress inspired by God was false, but went further and presented the contrary thesis that western history was going to a kind of frozen Hell. In doing so he simply set up another system against which the sober reacted. With only the extremes of extravagant optimism and pessimism to choose from, a generation of historians retreated to their libraries, safe in the conviction that the truth, as usual, lay somewhere in between. Adams's theory had a great deal in common with the economic emphasis of Beard and it is not surprising that Beard in 1943 should have called it one of the most important books of all time. Yet it was far more audacious than anything by Beard himself, for Adams not only developed a theory of history based on social, psychological, and economic factors, he advanced a cosmic chemistry as its basis. On the social level he maintained that western society had evolved from an era which was originally "martial," "emotional," "imaginative," and "artistic" to one in which the economic mind prevailed, and while the economic mind had expressed itself in several different historical types, its last and most petrifying expression was the usurer. The captains and the kings had truly departed, the artists and the priests had fled, and the usurer held reins which were thinly disguised purse strings. Only a reinfusion of barbarian emotion could save us from the gray death of finance capitalism.

For Brooks Adams all of this was merely the social expression of a more cosmic phenomenon. He did not develop it very far but something like it became the fundamental concern of his more famous brother Henry, so much so that Brooks modestly acknowledged that while he, Brooks, might have originated the theory, it was Henry who perfected it. And what did Henry do? Henry exploited for all it was worth that grim law, the second law of thermodynamics, which combined with the iron law of wages to cast a deterministic pall over the nineteenth century. The law says that in an isolated system with irreversible changes going on, heat energy tends to become less and less available for useful work. From it, with the help of numerous scientists and savants, Henry Adams concluded that the world would ultimately become cold and dead, that we were inexorably headed for a doom even more final than brother Brooks had described because at least Brooks held out the possibility of reviving hot-headed barbarism if only we could get hold of the proper serum.

The second law of thermodynamics was one which only Maxwell's demon could controvert, and so in the absence of demonic powers Henry Adams was led to prophetic pessimism and from there to seeking a law which would inscribe it by means of algebra in the hearts of men. The Adamses foresaw the tragedy and turmoil of the twentieth century but that gives credit to their political shrewdness and not to their theoretical genius. Successful scientific prediction is not just a matter of saying in advance what is then seen to be true, but also of formulating principles which clearly imply these true predictions, and this the Adamses did not do. Their history was better than their chemistry. In their hands the second law of thermodynamics was not a scientific theory to be confirmed and tested seriously but rather a stick with which to beat down the theological optimism of historians like Bancroft and, more important, the biological optimism of Spencerians and Darwinians who saw Evolution carrying us onward and upward.

American academic historians, with justice I think, remained profoundly suspicious of this kind of theorizing, much as they may have admired some of the substantive historical contributions which appear in the work of the Adamses. One should not be surprised, therefore, to hear one of the most eminent historians of his generation, Professor Samuel Eliot Morison, say: "Very early in my professional career I observed a certain frustration in a historian whom I greatly admired, Henry Adams, who had spent much time and thought searching for a 'law of history.' So I have cultivated the vast garden of human experience which is history, without troubling myself overmuch about laws, essential first causes, or how it is all coming out." Morison rejected not only the speculative philosophy of history he found in Henry Adams but also revived the famous formula of Ranke: that the task of the historian is to report the facts as they really are. Apparently Morison started to cultivate his garden after abandoning both of the more philosophical concerns of the American historian in the last half-century: the speculative cyclical theorizing of the Adamses and the obscure methodological pragmatism of a later generation of historians who followed Beard and Carl Becker. And while one cannot help sympathizing with his disappointment with Henry Adams's results, Morison's revival of Ranke invites scrutiny.

It is always refreshing to hear that the historian wants to report the facts as they really are — to tell the truth. But while it is easy enough to announce this as the function of the historian when the truth of isolated statements like 'Caesar crossed the Rubicon' is at stake, the matter is wholly different when we have to evaluate total histories or syntheses. All historians agree that Caesar crossed the Rubicon, but not all of them present the same "picture" of Rome. We like to say that some pictures of Rome are superior to others. Why? What is there about two pictures of an historical period that makes one better than the other in spite of the fact that both of them can be shown to be truthful in what they say? Morison complains that Beard's book *President Roosevelt and the Coming of the War, 1941* contains no single statement which can be isolated as false but that it somehow gives a false picture of the whole situation. We are tempted to introduce a counterpart to the legal concept of the whole truth and to try to discover which history comes closest to presenting it. But what is "the whole truth" about Rome or the coming of World War II? We cannot take the historical picture and compare it with a block of the past and see whether it accurately depicts that block. We seem to be committed to the metaphor of an historical picture and yet not able to exploit any of its advantages, hence the disappointment with the picture theory of historical syntheses and the flight to pragmatism.

Pragmatism, however, has its own troubles and it won't do to apply it too crudely to the present situation. It won't do to point out that every history is written with the intention of solving problems growing out of present needs and then to conclude that satisfaction of these needs constitutes the truth of the historical picture, for we want to say that no matter how much the rewriting of history satisfies political needs the result is not a true historical account of what happened. Neither will it do to remind us that we get interested in certain aspects of history as a result of certain needs in ourselves and our times. We all know that we try to study what interests us and that this selection of problems goes on in the natural sciences as well as in history. But this is not the kind of selection which creates the fundamental puzzle of the philosophy of history. That puzzle is created by our persisting in the conviction that there is something called the whole truth about the period or event we are studying, that we can never speak this whole truth, that histories are good to the extent to which they approximate this whole truth, and therefore that some selections or approximations are objectively better than others.

At this point it is easy to be attracted to a view which emphasizes the esthetic element in history. Since we speak of pictures why not say that an historical picture is to be judged in the way we judge a Rembrandt or a Botticelli? And yet, no matter how much style determines our admiration of histories, isn't it grotesque to suppose that assessing an historical work is *just like* judging a painting or a novel? The historian doesn't busily verify all of his isolated statements while they are on little cards and proceed to paste them together just for esthetic effect; moreover the combination with the best esthetic effect is often avoided by good historians in favor of something else. Many a history would be more artfully constructed if its author had carefully burned some of these little cards or replaced them with others. Yet we don't advise historians to carry on in this way unless they want to write romances or campaign biographies.

It is hard to avoid the conclusion that narrative should be the central concern of the theorist of historical knowledge, just because narration is the most typical activity of the historian. Of course the historian does other things as well, in fact does them in the course of developing a narrative. He offers causal explanations, and reports on isolated details of history. But the historian is *more* than a reporter of isolated past detail and a seeker of causes. If he were nothing more, the logic of his discipline might be divided and parceled out to the various branches of general philosophy. But precisely because contemporary philosophers of language tend to concentrate on the logic of *single* statements — whether statements about the past, explanatory statements, logical statements, scientific theories, or moral judgments — they overlook the narrative, which is a special kind of discourse deserving of special treatment. If we succeed in clarifying the logic of narration, we shall have inaugurated a new era in the philosophy of history with the help of the tools of linguistic philosophy. No longer will the philosophy of history be a poor relative in the community of philosophical disciplines, occasionally visited by those bent on proving that history is disguised sociology, politics, fiction, or ethics. For narrative history is a unique form of human discourse and those who study it are entitled to a house on the hill.

7 ·

Historical Inevitability

Sɪʀ Isaiah Berlin's brilliant essay *Historical Inevitability* *
is the product of an unusual combination of qualities in its
author, a remarkable thinker who combines the logico-analytic
skill that we associate with the tradition of Bertrand Russell,
G. E. Moore, and Ludwig Wittgenstein, with the historical
insight and sensibility that are more usually associated with
historians and philosophers in the Continental tradition. Berlin's versatility reflects his own history, which is that of a
Russian who was brought to England in his childhood, who
became an influential friend of the philosophical revolution
that has converted Oxford into the center of linguistic philosophy it is today, and who is now one of the world's most
distinguished historians of Russian thought, the author of a
biography of Karl Marx and of *The Hedgehog and the Fox*, a
scintillating book on Tolstoi's philosophy of history.

In his study of Tolstoi Berlin first produced his suggestive
contrast between the hedgehog — the man who knows one
big thing, who has one central idea which organizes his beliefs
and experiences, who has a large, rich vision of the kind that
we associate with the great systematic metaphysicians — and
the fox — the careful, meticulous, analytical student of profound and relevant detail. Tolstoi, Mr. Berlin suggested, "was

* Oxford University Press, Oxford, 1954.

· 75 ·

by nature a fox, but believed in being a hedgehog," and my own hypothesis is that Mr. Berlin is by nature a hedgehog who fortunately believes in being a fox. This, I think, may illuminate his bold but carefully reasoned book, the first Auguste Comte Memorial Trust Lecture, delivered at the London School of Economics in 1953.

The philosophical world (outside of Oxford) first knew of Mr. Berlin as the author of articles on logical problems surrounding induction and on the positivist criterion of meaning, also as a name in the preface of A. J. Ayer's *Language, Truth and Logic*, where he was thanked for having gone over every point of that flaming manifesto against metaphysics. For all that the reading public could tell, Berlin was one of those clever, logically-minded young men of the 1930's who felt the beneficial effect of logical positivism, who were trying to rid philosophy of the muddles of two thousand years, and who constituted a cadre of tough analysts, bent on pricking the bubbles of speculative philosophy, preoccupied with sense-data, and constantly minding the '*p*'s and '*q*'s of *Principia Mathematica*. They formed a no-nonsense school, a logical school, and empirical school, a school of foxes. It came as a distinct surprise, therefore, to those who knew of Berlin only by way of footnotes, prefaces, and articles in the *Proceedings of the Aristotelian Society*, to hear of the publication of his *Karl Marx: His Life and Environment* in 1939. For what could be further from one's conception of a logical analyst than a biographer of such a turbulent subject? Does one think of Moore writing a life of Marx? Or Wittgenstein? One knows of Russell's books on marriage, war, peace, freedom, and socialism; one knows of Whitehead's brilliant histories of ideas. But a biography by either one of them is unthinkable, because biography requires the kind of interest in individual people, in their motives and feelings, which we do not associate with the logician's temperament. Berlin's book on Marx indicated, therefore, that he was an unusual philosopher in the English-speaking world, that he was deeply, and not just abstractly, concerned with the lives of active, suffering human beings. Moreover, it revealed a preoccupation with that very un-English, very Russian subject, the philosophy of history, and a familiarity with Continental thought and culture that one might easily understand in an idealist or phenomenologist but which seemed odd in an English friend of logical positivism.

After the biography of Marx appeared, the war brought Berlin to Washington on a government mission, and there he is said to have produced a series of astonishingly penetrating reports on the American scene which were admired by all who read them, notably by Churchill. Since then his lectures at Oxford and Harvard on the history of Russian thought, his little book on Tolstoi, his studies of his favorite Belinsky, and his widely discussed Third Programme talks on romantic political theory have made it clear that he is one of the most original and interesting minds on the English scene. Moreover, they make it obvious that the logical Berlin of the 1930's was a hedgehog beneath the skin, a man of large, expansive, humanistic concerns who was confining himself to a genre that was too tight and restrictive for someone with his historical, political, and literary talents. This is one reason why the book under review is of special interest. In it Berlin picks up his logical tools once again, but this time he applies them to problems in a boggy field which is too often the preserve of pure hedgehogs, hedgehogs with no sense of logic. In approaching the philosophy of history with the devices of a logical analyst, Berlin confirms one's hopeful suspicion that for all of his magnificently cascading sentences and in spite of his extraordinary genius at painting large, sweeping pictures of men and ages, he will never abandon his interest in reasoning carefully, sharply, and clearly. It is in this sense that he believes in being a fox and this is what makes him unique among historians and cultural critics today.

The main purpose of Berlin's lecture is to refute the doctrine of complete determinism. Its epigraph, "those vast impersonal forces," is taken from T. S. Eliot's *Notes towards the Definition of Culture*, and it is against the notion that we are all in the tight grip of such mysterious powers that Berlin argues in a most devastating way. But the proponents of such forces are not the only ones attacked by Berlin, since he is on the trail of more modest determinists too. He is also shooting at those who, although they are just as vehement as he is in denouncing occult forces, maintain that all our choices are determined by causes of a less nebulous kind. For the sober determinist these causes are not as colossal and vaporous as Hegel's World Spirit, but that is not enough of a retreat or concession for Berlin. He insists over and over again that some of our choices must be regarded as free in the sense that no forces or causes whatever, whether they be vast and impersonal or tiny and personal, produce these choices. He will not be satisfied with saying that we are free only in the sense that we can often do as we choose, that no shadow will fall between the choice and the act. He insists that at least some of our choices are themselves free, that is to say, uncaused and therefore unpredictable by scientific means. And his chief argument for this view rests on his contention that praising or blaming an action requires it to be free in this unqualified sense. "If I were convinced that although choices did affect what occurred, yet they were themselves wholly determined by factors not within the individual's control . . . , I should not regard him as morally praiseworthy or blameworthy."

Berlin's chief point, as is evident from this quotation, is that complete determinism is incompatible with what ordinary men and historians believe in their sane and sober moments: that we are sometimes morally praised and blamed and are therefore responsible for some of our actions. If all of our choices were determined, none of our actions would be morally judgeable, which consequence Berlin says is absurd.

In the face of such an inconsistency between determinism and moral judgment we might think ourselves free to choose either one of the horns of the dilemma, for example, determinism. But this is impossible, according to Berlin. He thinks of complete determinism as an expendable philosophical doctrine, but he regards the fact of praise and blame as an inescapable part of our way of thinking and speaking. In such a case, he says, there is no alternative but to give up the offending philosophical doctrine. One might almost say that according to Berlin we are forced to praise and blame, and therefore forced to regard ourselves as free. (There is irony here, but not inconsistency, since Berlin does not say that all of our choices are free.)

The two main problems raised by Berlin's argument are these: (1) Are moral judgment and complete determinism logically incompatible? and (2) Is the language of praise and blame, in contrast to determinism, an inescapable part of our thinking process? Let us consider the first question first. Is it logically inconsistent to praise or blame an action that we believe to have been determined by things outside of the agent's control? If we do praise or blame such an action, is that like saying, 'All men are mortal, Socrates is a man, but Socrates is *not* mortal', or 'Five is an odd number and five is not an odd number'? I think not, although Berlin seems to think it is. For my own part, I think that someone who blames an action of this kind is doing something that we may find morally objectionable but certainly not logically inconsistent. If we believe that a man has done something that is determined by causes beyond his control, we think it not illogical to blame him, but nasty, cruel, wrong, unfeeling. We think he does not *deserve* censure. And what this shows, I think, is that we have to do here not with the violation of a logical principle, as Berlin seems to think, but rather with the violation of a moral principle.

What is the bearing of this on Mr. Berlin's main thesis? It suggests, I think, that his attempt to move from the fact that certain acts are praiseworthy or blameworthy to the conclusion that some choices are free itself presupposes some such moral principle as 'Only acts chosen freely *deserve* praise or blame'. Once this is made explicit, we see why the matter is so difficult and controversial, for it is fair to say that convergence on this moral principle is rarer than convergence on logical principles. What is at stake is something that distinguishes different ways of life (to use a phrase which is as helpful here as it is banal). "Is it morally wrong?" we should ask, and not, "Is it logically absurd?" to blame a man for some hideous crime, even though we believe he was caused to do it. Berlin says that "If we are told that a given case of stealing is due to kleptomania, we protest that the appropriate treatment is not punishment but a remedy for a disease." And yet think of Hitler. How many were there who sought remedies for his head rather than his head itself?

So far I have not discussed the second question raised earlier: Is the language of praise and blame, in contrast to determinism, an inescapable part of our thinking process? It seems to me that we must acknowledge, as Berlin does not, that the principle of complete determinism is deeply ingrained in the thinking habits of some men. Universal causation has its own independent support, and it is doubtful whether even its being logically incompatible with moral praise and blame would dislodge it from the minds of some men. Think, therefore, how much less forceful Berlin's argument becomes when it is said, as I am prepared to say, that the principle which makes determinism and moral judgment incompatible is itself a moral principle which we can accept or reject. We may then view the whole situation in a much more fluid way. Those who think deterministically can change if they wish to; those who pass moral judgments can give up that activity; and the moral principle that makes it wrong to pass moral judgment on determined acts might be surrendered. What the matter somes down to, I think, is a choice among several consistent systems of belief and practice. Berlin recognizes the abstract possibility of viewing all human actions in an esthetic way, much as we view paintings, poems, and sunsets. We admire them or find them ugly even though we believe them to be caused, or the products of artists whose choices might be determined. I must confess that, unlike Berlin, I can imagine a way of life which accepts universal causation, maintains the principle that "ought" implies "can" (in its moral version), and refrains from giving out moral marks; I can imagine Berlin's way of life, in which one gives up universal causation, mantains the principle that "ought" implies "can," and passes judgment only on those acts which are free. I can imagine accepting any of the other self-consistent triads.

The first serious question that immediately arises is: Which triad represents our way of life? To this Berlin's answer is simple: it is the one I have called his in the preceding paragraph. But even if it were, one should want to ask whether it should be, and yet Berlin almost thinks it silly for us to raise this question, since he says that we are psychologically forced into the language of praise and blame, that giving it up is psychologically impossible. But there is a point at which Berlin says: "I do not here wish to say that determinism is necessarily false, only that we neither speak nor think as if it could be true." And when one adds to this his statement that we are forced to speak and think in ways that are incompatible with determinism, one wonders whether Berlin is willing to accept a certain grim consequence of his two statements: that we might be forced to speak falsely, which is to say that determinism might be true even though we were unable to speak as though it was. Now I do not deny that the triad to which Berlin subscribes might be the most acceptable of them all. But if I affirmed that it was, I should not defend it as Berlin does. The fact that I give moral marks does not seem to me an unalterable fact of my psychology, nor do I think that the principle that we should not judge unfree acts is inescapable.

Any one of the elements in what I have called Berlin's way of life might be surrendered. Some may seem more stable than others, but this is no guarantee of permanent immunity. In describing one's way of life in this manner one makes it clear that one is free to change it, at one's own peril of course; one also avoids the irony of Berlin's position, which is that of saying that we are forced to regard ourselves as free.

In arguing as I have, I find myself disagreeing with one of the things that Berlin says, and agreeing with another, which makes me suspect an inconsistency in his lecture. In his more rigid mood he says: "My submission is that to make a serious attempt to adapt our words to the hypothesis of determinism is scarcely feasible, as things are now, and have been within recorded history. The changes involved are too radical; our moral categories are, in the end, little more flexible than our physical ones; we cannot begin to think out in real terms, to which behavior and speech would correspond, what the universe of the genuine determinist would be like, any more than we can think out, with the minimum of indispensable concrete detail (i. e. begin to imagine) what it would be like to be in a timeless world, or one with a seventeen-dimensional space" (p. 34). In his less rigid mood, the one I find more congenial, Berlin says: "All our categories are, in theory, subject to change. The physical categories — e.g. the three dimensions and infinite extent of ordinary perceptual space, the irreversibility of temporal processes, the multiplicity and countability of material objects — are perhaps the most fixed. Yet even a shift in these most general characteristics is in principle conceivable. After these come orders and relations of sensible qualities — colours, shapes, tastes, etc.; then the uniformities on which the sciences are based — these can be quite easily thought away in fairy tales or scientific romances. The categories of value are more fluid than these; and within them tastes fluctuate more than rules of etiquette, and these more than moral standards" (p. 56n).

My submission is that the second passage quoted is philosophically sounder than the first, and that it goes a long way toward contradicting the notion, stated so often in this lecture, that determinism is psychologically impossible. Moreover, in the second passage Berlin implies that moral categories are "more fluid" than physical categories while in the first he says that they are "little more flexible" than physical categories.

At this point we reach a matter which leads very naturally to the other main question of Berlin's essay: historical relativism. Unfortunately I have spent so much of my space on his exciting discussion of determination that I cannot consider his profound dissection of relativism here. I hope that my disagreements with him on some of the matters considered will not obscure my estimate of his total contribution. In my opinion, this essay of Berlin's is one of the most brilliant and provocative studies in the philosophy of history to have appeared in many years. Where one disagrees with him, one feels that further discussion would certainly narrow the gap, for one knows that one is dealing with a thinker whose interest in man and the cosmos is equaled by his respect for logic: in short, that Isaiah Berlin is a hedgehog who believes in being a fox.

8 ·

Religion, Politics, and the Higher Learning

AMONG religious intellectuals today the most important question, the question that exercises them most even when it is not asked in this form, is not 'Does God exist?' but rather 'Should I be religious?' And this reformulation has been the source of both liberation and confusion, particularly in the sphere of higher education, where it has become increasingly fashionable to urge the importance of religious instruction for the undergraduate. If you adopt the more traditional way of stating the religious question you cannot avoid asking yourself what evidence there is for belief in God or what arguments there are for the existence of God, and even if you say you have faith, you may be fairly asked why you have faith. If, however, you defend faith as a policy, you may be asked to supply evidence for the statement that it is an advisable policy, and once again you will be involved in a logical argument, that is to say, one in which you claim to know or believe something and therefore one in which you may be fairly asked to defend your claim or your belief. Now there is no doubt that a large and increasing number of religious intellectuals do not feel, or at any rate, do not say, that arguments of either kind are relevant to their religious beliefs. They do not use traditional proofs of God's existence and are not likely to be moved by a request for a justification of faith. What, then, do they believe?

Obviously not the simple, old-fashioned declarative statement of theology, that God exists, for then they might feel some compulsion to give arguments for what is not obvious to everyone. A reasonable suggestion is that they believe a moral statement for which they are willing to argue: that one should, or one ought, or that it is good, to be religious. In other words, the serious question to which they address themselves is the second one we have mentioned: 'Should I be religious?'

The educational implications of this transformation of the religious question are serious enough. Those who wish to introduce religious instruction into the undergraduate college and who adopt this more recent way of construing religion must now ask themselves just what they mean by religion. Having abandoned the straightforward and simple definition of a religious man as one who believes in God and defends his belief, they must set forth an alternative view. The twentieth century has witnessed a number of efforts to redefine religion in the light of this religious distaste for traditional theology; they vary from an excessively narrow view of the religious life as a life of feeling (as opposed to knowing) to one that rightly regards religion as a total way of life — cognitive, esthetic, affective, moral, and even political. The first alternative is untrue to religion, as I shall try to argue in this necessarily brief essay on an enormous subject, while the second, if acted upon by those who are responsible in these matters, will be untrue to the aims of undergraduate education. In this respect it is like instruction in (rather than on) Communism.

Of the three analogous questions that may be formulated by using the words 'religious', 'moral', and 'scientific', 'Should I be religious?' is probably the only one that is significant. Its counterparts 'Should I be moral?' (meaning by that 'Should I do what is right?') and 'Should I be scientific?' (meaning by that 'Should I use the devices of experiment, observation, and deduction when I try to find out something about the world?') have a *prima facie* emptiness about them which is confirmed by philosophical reflection. But 'Should I be religious?' is of an entirely different order. It is meaningful and momentous, as William James said. It is the kind of question that even a clever philosopher would have difficulty in proving meaningless. But while it is surely not meaningless, it is not easy to say what it means.

The history of the shift from asking bluntly, without 'if's and 'but's, 'Does God exist?' to asking 'Should I be religious?' is the history of the philosophy of religion in our time. George Santayana is as important a figure in its development as anyone in the twentieth century. He quotes Bacon's aphorism "A little philosophy inclineth a man's mind to atheism but depth in philosophy bringeth men's minds to religion," and the jump from the word 'atheism' to the word 'religion' is symbolic of the transformation I have in mind. The point is that atheism is the belief in the nonexistence of God (or the nonbelief in the existence of God), while religion is, for Santayana, not theism. But if depth in philosophy bringeth one to religion, one must go even deeper to find out what the word 'religion' means.

I do not think that the traditional differences over the nature of God are any greater than recent philosophical differences about the nature of religion. Religion has meant all things to all philosophers and that is one reason why the modern transformation of the religious question has been confusing as well as liberating. Having escaped the difficult logic of theologians, religious intellectuals with no taste for scholastic disputation must now face the perplexing question 'What is religion?' In the nineteenth century it was fashionable to say that one knew that there was a God but that His nature was mysterious and unknowable. But plainly one cannot take the analogous way out when discussing the nature of religion. One cannot say 'I know that religion exists but its nature is mysterious'.

The answers to the question 'What is religion?' have come trippingly in the twentieth century. It is a species of poetry (Santayana); it is a variety of shared experience (Dewey); it is ethical culture; it is insight into man's nature. (The last is the view of a group that might be called "Atheists for Niebuhr.") In short, being religious, as one might expect, is not the sort of attribute that one can identify easily by the method of genus and differentia: it is not immediately susceptible to the analytic methods that G. E. Moore has used on brotherhood ("To be a brother is to be a male sibling"), nor is it easily treated by the powerful definitional techniques of mathematical logic. What too many philosophers tend to suppose — wrongly — is that examples of religious behavior have a property in common, that we can easily identify it, and that the disputes of philosophers are differences about the essence or analysis of this property. But granting that this is a simple-minded view of the matter, is there no unity in all of the different aspects upon which different philosophers have seized? Even if none of their proposed definitions presents "the essence" of the religious life, is there nothing which they reflect that may help us formulate a more complex and therefore more adequate view of religion?

One answer is that they all reveal a desire that underlies a vast amount of contemporary talk about religion: the desire, not only to avoid identifying religion with belief in one single assertion, such as 'God exists', but to avoid identifying religion with any claim to knowledge that might have to run the gauntlet of scientific test. (One might be tempted to except those who identify religion with insight into human nature, and therefore with something like psychology, but atheists for Niebuhr, like Niebuhr himself, think of their insight as transcending scientific psychology.) In other words, the various oversimplifications of religion — whether they make it mean just appreciating poetry, or just living in community, or just adopting a certain moral code, or just having the insights of a Kierkegaard, a Dostoevsky, or a Pascal — are negatively motivated. They are dominated by a desire to make religion fill the void created by the dissolving effects of science, both physical, as at Hiroshima, and spiritual. This has been one outcome of the nineteenth century's hot war between science and religion. It has ended in an uncomfortable cease-fire and in the creation of a line that would separate knowledge from all other human activities. Religion has too often agreed to accept the role of a nonscientific spiritual grab bag or of an ideological know-nothing, while science has promised to give up its control over feeling and will.

Several observations are in order. First of all, it is plain that the various efforts to identify religion with poetry, community, liturgy, or morality by themselves are as misguided as the identification of religion with assent to one abstract proposition. Religion is not any one of these taken by itself. Religion is most faithfully viewed as a compound of all of these elements.

In Wittgenstein's phrase, they may all have deep family re-semblances that distinguish them from science, but religion is a holy family composed of all of these concerns rather than any one of them by itself. Moreover, no seriously religious person can combine the liturgy of Roman Catholicism, the ethics of Judaism, and the Protestant theory of man. The result would be a spiritual monstrosity. And while their connections are not logical, like those between the axioms and theorems of a mathematical system, the elements of religion have organic connections with each other that make it more difficult to mix them modishly as we mix different styles of furniture. They make up a cultural pattern, and therefore cannot be torn apart and reassembled into homemade jalopies with Ford engines and Cadillac bodies. They may die when they are transplanted or when spiritual Burbanks begin their grafting. Revolutionary and hybrid religions may come into being, but they become real and moving for ordinary people only after heretics and reformers have created interesting new spiritual collages with the remnants of the past and items of the present.

It follows that we must go one step further in our transfor-mation of the religious question. If we ask it at all, we should not ask abstractly 'Should I be religious?' but rather 'Should I be a Jew?' or 'Should I be a Roman Catholic?' or 'Should I be a Protestant?' And when we have asked one of these more specific questions, the further question is bound to arise: must we not go back to asking, among other things, whether God exists, as He is conceived by these different religions? I suggest now that it is not only pointless to ask the question 'Should I be religious?' without specifying a particular religion, but that we cannot disengage the purely affective and active elements of that religion from its cognitive or putatively cognitive elements. Even if theology be treated as myth, as Santayana treats it, it is different from the explicitly liturgical, poetic, moral, and social aspects of religion even though not separate from them. It is impossible, I suggest, to be a Jew in any serious way without accepting the Judaic picture of God, or to be a Christian without forming an image of Christ consonant with Christian ritual and morality. I must emphasize the fact that this is not a matter of logical impossibility. Clearly we may accept a large part of what is called Christian ethics without being forced deductively to accept its theological underpinnings if only because one does not imply the other as the axioms of Euclid imply his theorems. That is almost obvious. But what is quite obvious is the fact that esthetic attitudes toward stained glass and Gregorian chant are possible in the absence of any great respect for St. Thomas' proofs of the existence of God. If you admire the windows and the chants you may admire them as elements of the religious culture that inspires them, but you are not *ipso facto* a religious man. Moreover, this is no time to say that the artist sees the essence of Christianity better than the priest, or that we should redefine 'religion' as the biologist redefines 'fish' to suit our present purposes.

It is for the acute anthropologist, the cultural historian, and the sensitive philosopher to tell us something about these difficult, nonlogical connections between a given theology, its poetry, and its associated customs. Recent philosophers of language have tried to say something about the connection between factual statements and value statements, but illuminating as it is, it is not enough for our purposes. What we need is insight into a connection which is even more unlike logical implication than the relation between fact and value, because it does not bind statements to statements, but statements to feelings, tastes, customs, attitudes, and action. Whatever it turns out to be on closer inspection, it underlies those compulsions and impulses which are uniquely associated with particular theologies, the compulsions that lead us to swallow our religions whole.

I suggest, therefore, that the cease-fire proposed by the twentieth century for the war of the nineteenth, the attempt to arbitrate the nineteenth-century struggle by granting science a sphere of influence over knowledge and religion a sharply separated sphere of influence over feeling and will, is unworkable and necessarily unstable. For being religious in the sense of the question 'Should I be religious?' involves commitment on all levels of experience, including one that is cognitive or taken to be cognitive by the religious man. Far from catering to the whole man in whose interest the cease-fire is often signed, the compromise view of religion as a purely emotive, or esthetic, or social affair encourages the most far-reaching kind of fragmentation. It is instructively ironic that Deism, the one great serious attempt to distill a nonhistorical essence of religion, has been purely intellectual in its emphasis. The effort of Lord Herbert of Cherbury to extract the core of all religions by listing its fundamental truths as: "(1) That God exists, (2) that it is a duty to worship Him, (3) that the practice of virtue is the true mode of doing Him honor, (4) that man is under the obligation to repent of his sins, and (5) that there will be rewards and punishments after death," * became the tradition of the Enlightenment, the period which has been attacked so violently by our darker theorists of religion. And the Enlightenment, as the author who summarizes Lord Herbert's view points out, was not as interested in a "searching analysis of the living religious experience" as our latter-day philosophers of religion are. It was highly intellectualistic in its approach to religion and yet it failed to distill its theoretical essence. Think, therefore, how much more difficult it will be for those who identify religion with "the living religious experience" to propose an analysis of religion in abstraction from the living experiences and theological beliefs of Jew or Gentile. In a sense the newer, antirationalistic view of religion merely makes the reverse error of the Enlightenment. It concentrates on feeling and will while the Enlightenment was fixed on the intellect in its attempt to define religion.

I come at last to the implications of these reflections for higher education, and I suggest that any educational effort to nourish religious feeling or to stimulate religious action by trying to present an abstract essence of religion, conceived as the life of feeling and willing (as opposed to knowing), will fail. From this I conclude that we should not make the effort in colleges which are not religious institutions, and that we become frankly sectarian in our teaching of religion and therefore limit higher religious instruction to the divinity schools; since divinity schools are more properly devoted to the *study and the propagation* of religions conceived as total ways of life, knowledge, emotion, and action.

* G. C. Joyce, "Deism," Hastings' *Encyclopedia of Religion and Ethics*, Vol. 4, p. 533.

Plainly, it does not follow that we must abandon the effort to help undergraduates to develop their emotions, to find themselves, to help them develop habits of practical decision, and to appreciate humane values. These are certainly admissible concerns of all scholars and can very easily be the major concern of those who choose to do that sort of thing while they teach Plato and Shakespeare, Dostoevsky and Epicurus, Kant and Pascal. Certainly the history of religion can be adorned with this kind of feeling if the teacher is willing to do it and able to communicate the truth while he does it. But teaching *about* religion, or communicating moral feeling and esthetic appreciation while one teaches philosophy, literature, and history, no more constitutes teaching people to *be* religious in any ordinary sense of that word, than teaching *about* Communism amounts to propagating it. To teach people to be religious, I repeat, we must do something which is beyond the function of an undergraduate college simply because it involves inculcating a total appreciation of and belief in historical religions treated as the vast, all-embracing structures that they are. But are we prepared to lecture in Judaism 7, Catholicism 8, and Protestantism 9?

My point may be made a little clearer by comparing the teacher of feeling and willing with the teacher of knowing, and I select as an example of the latter the physics professor as the pre-eminent teacher of knowing in our time. When he is teaching science as opposed to the history of science, to the college student, the physicist must believe or pretend to believe the theory he teaches; and if he doesn't believe it, as teachers of elementary physics might not, at least he must justify his noble pedagogical lie at some point in the young physicist's scientific education. Newton's theory may come first without the necessary qualifications, but when Einstein's is presented the student should come to see the sense in which the latter supersedes the former — either by outright refutation or by absorption as a special case. What is the religious parallel to this total involvement of the physics professor in, say, theory of relativity, or quantum theory? Total involvement in one of the religions, I imagine. But if we are not willing, as many are not, to teach the undergraduate religion in this way, because it is not our proper function, can we justify teaching what might seem like the religious counterpart to courses in the history and methodology of science? In other words, are there subjects that stand in relation to the different religions as general methodology does to the individual sciences? There are. For example, there is the history of religion, comparative religion, anthropology of religion, a course in the philosophy of religion, or, if a genius is available to teach it, a course in general religion which will embrace all of these and more synoptically. But will such wholly justifiable courses teach people to *be* religious in the way that concentration in physics should teach people to *be* physicists? No, and for the same reason that courses in general methodology don't teach people to be scientists. At best the course in methodology of science gives the interested student an introduction to the spirit of science, but surely nothing that makes him a scientist. He may come to feel something of what the scientific life is like, but if he has not had serious contact with some one science and lived in it for even a short time, no amount of methodological tourism will make him a scientist or scientifically minded. The parallel in the case of religion is obvious. If it should be said after all this that religious instruction is not supposed to make people religious, but simply to give them some understanding of the religious life, that can be achieved, not by teaching students how to feel and act religiously, but by teaching them what they should know about religious feeling, action, and belief. If in absorbing this knowledge students develop deep religious feelings, it will happen *per accidens*, as it were, and not as a result of the concerted efforts of the professors of feeling and willing.

If the comparison with science does not illuminate the matter, perhaps an analogy with politics will. Take, for example, the current debate over whether the colleges should offer courses *on* Communism as opposed to courses *in* Communism. Isn't this an illuminating parallel to the question whether we should offer courses *in* religion rather than *on* it? The one great difference — our abhorrence of Communism — is irrelevant to the issue we are considering here. The important point is that Communism is very close to a religion, with its theology (dialectical materialism), its conception of community (the dictatorship of the proletariat), its myth and its liturgy (Red Square, Stalin's pictures, and Lenin's Tomb), and its poetry. And if we should give lessons *in* Communism we should be going beyond our function as teachers in a college, just as we should if we should try to give lessons in Judaism, Catholicism, or Protestantism. Those who know the defects of Communism have an extra argument in the hole, but the card that shows is enough and in a sense more powerful for our purposes. Communism, like all of the traditional religions, should not be propagated in educational institutions which are not fundamentally devoted to the advancement of

Communism, Judaism, Christianity, or Mohammedanism, though all of them should be studied objectively in their many different aspects. That is the fundamental point.

I do not believe that the struggle between the free world and Russia may be glibly identified as a struggle between Christianity and Communism, or that one cannot fight Soviet tyranny effectively without being religious; but if either of these contentions were true, they would merely accentuate the importance of studying both Communism and traditional religion objectively in the undergraduate college. In studying religion the student will be studying something for which he will be sympathetically prepared but which he may not understand; in studying Communism he will be studying something he may oppose but also fail to understand. The function of a teacher of undergraduates in any institution which is not dominated by religious aims is to study and analyze both religion and Communism. We should not be excessively Spinozistic on the point and say that we must neither laugh nor cry, but *only* understand. We may laugh about one and cry about the other, but our central function is understanding and the communication of that understanding to our students.

I should not like to end on a note that depends on the difficult notion of *central function*, for colleges are man-made and their functions may be changed by men, especially men who can turn plowshares into swords and electrons into bombs. But we must remember that the colleges and the universities have lived through crises before, and that some of the severest blows at their greatness and their usefulness as social institutions have come when it seemed necessary to change their function under the influence of religious or political passion.

9 ·

Religious Commitment and Higher Education

THE main concern of the previous essay was undergraduate religious instruction. In the present essay I should like to offer a few related reflections and proposals on the distinct, but closely connected, problem of instruction in a divinity school which is part of a large university. I have no particular divinity school and no particular university in mind and my proposals may be utopian, but I wish to exercise the philosopher's right to sketch an ideal which, I hope, is not too remote to be carried out some day. To my limited knowledge it has not yet been tried in a serious way.

In the previous essay I argued that religions represent total ways of life, patterns of thought, feeling, and action, and therefore that teaching someone to be religious not only aims at conveying knowledge, but also at inducing him to adopt certain moral and esthetic attitudes, certain views of man and society, and possibly even certain political beliefs. I therefore maintained that if religions are such total and intricately woven cultural configurations, religious instruction is likely to be specific. That is to say, those who aspire to teach someone to be religious are likely to teach him to be a Jew, a Catholic, or a Protestant, for example. "The attempt to speak without speaking any particular language," says Santayana, "is not more hopeless than the attempt to have a religion that shall be no religion in particular."

· 98 ·

I concluded that such religious persuasion should not be attempted by any college which was not denominational in the narrowest sense, for unless the faculty of such a college were prepared to endorse and advocate one religion as *the* true religion, it would have no good reason for inculcating the precepts and practices of that religion alone. I maintained, moreover, that the distinction between teaching an undergraduate to *be* religious and teaching him *about* religion was cardinal and that this, in another sphere, was precisely the distinction drawn by those who do not confuse instruction *in* Communism with instruction *about* Communism. Instruction *about* many religions is an indispensable part of any educational program, but it is wrong, I argued, to expect a college to offer courses *in* many different religions. Not only because of the difficulty of deciding on generally acceptable grounds which religion or religions to teach but, and this was the more important reason, because it is not the function of such an undergraduate college as I was considering to inculcate that vast unity of belief, feeling, and action which we identify with a religion. In passing I urged that we limit instruction in religion to schools of divinity and theology since they are properly devoted to the study and the propagation of religions conceived as total ways of life, knowledge, emotion, and action.

In this essay I wish to develop this last point further and to raise a number of questions connected with the view that a professor in the divinity school of a large and predominantly secular university should be what is sometimes called a committed man. I shall begin with the second matter for it will lead very naturally into the first.

Can a teacher give instruction — excellent instruction —

about a given religion without being committed to that religion? Can a scholar successfully study a given religion without being committed to that religion? The questions may be answered simply by appealing to the history of education and scholarship. Scholars and students of an earlier generation will recall George Foote Moore's great studies of Judaism and those in our own day will think of Harry Austyn Wolfson's great work on the philosophy of the Church Fathers. Such scholars and teachers answer our questions immediately and affirmatively, for neither of them accepted the religious doctrines they studied and taught about so brilliantly. Indeed, so affirmatively do Moore and Wolfson answer our questions that it is hard to know what is meant by those who maintain that one must be committed to a given religion in order to study it and to teach about it fully. Their error is just the reverse of those who say that an objective study of a religion can only be made by those who reject it. But this is just as erroneous as the contention that the only satisfactory teacher-scholar is one who adopts, who is committed to, the views he describes and analyzes. We are obviously in no position to generalize in this respect. There have been great Catholic students of Catholic theology and great non-Catholic students of it; there have been great Protestant students of Jewish theology; there have been great Jewish students of Catholic theology. All of the permutations can be illustrated. Moreover, I am told that the greatest scholars of certain Oriental religions are not adherents of those religions. I repeat that we are not in a position to generalize in this area, neither in regard to successful scholarship, nor in regard to effective teaching. And because we cannot generalize we would do well not to set up tests for professors which would require them to be for or require them to be against the religions or theologies they wish to deal with in an objective, scholarly way.

The point involved transcends the controversial cases of religion and politics. It applies to the case of the non-Aristotelian philosopher lecturing on Aristotle, to that of the professor of English who rejects Emerson's transcendentalism but who studies his work fully and lectures brilliantly on him, to the historian of Mohammedanism who is not a Mohammedan, to the Byzantinist who does not belong to the Greek Orthodox Church, to the anthropologist who is not a Zuni. In matters of scholarship and teaching *about* religion, literature, politics, philosophy, sociology, or morals, the doctrine "Credo ut intellegam" has no standing. We can understand Marxism without believing in it, we can understand Catholicism without believing in it, we can understand Judaism without believing in it, we can understand Protestantism without believing in it — certainly in that sense of the word 'understand' which is relevant to teaching and scholarship in our free, secular colleges and universities. A scholar and teacher must insist that it is possible to understand a statement without accepting it, to understand a style of literature without admiring it, to understand the motives of Napoleon, Caesar, or Stalin without praising them. Even if he should hold with Collingwood and Dilthey that such understanding requires putting one's self in the place of the men whose views one studies, a scholar need not literally adopt the views and attitudes of those whom he studies.

These remarks are intended to show — if there is any doubt about it — that at least one important part of the instruction offered in a divinity school or a school of theology need not be given by those who are committed to the religion they study, for one important part of such instruction is historical and therefore objective in intent. I turn now to a more difficlut question.

Must a teacher of *systematic* theology as opposed to a historian of religion in a divinity school which is part of a predominantly secular university be committed to a specific religion in order to pursue his studies and teaching successfully? No question is of greater importance, for its answer will determine whether and why a professor of divinity occupies a position unlike that of other professors in the university.

At first sight one might argue that commitment is belief in God, theology is the science of God, therefore a theologian will have to believe in the existence of God just as an astronomer will have to believe in the existence of heavenly bodies. There is a certain amount of dialectical power in this point (Would we ask someone who denied the existence of stars to teach astronomy?), but its power decreases directly with the distance between a religion which is dogmatic and authoritarian, and one which is more loosely knit. That is to say, where the conception of God is fixed by institutional authority or by sacred text in an unequivocal way the standard of commitment is only too clear. But where, for example, the divinity school is generally Protestant, where the very notion of God may vary with the professor who teaches systematic theology, the notion of commitment becomes ambiguous and shifting. The variation is likely to be so great that one man's God may be another's Devil. I dare say that many who think of themselves as committed might have such feelings about Professor Tillich's "God above the God of theism." What becomes of religious commitment then? Is there a univocal conception of it which will at one and the same time cover commitment to the God of theism and commitment to the God above Him? I doubt it. By reflecting on such questions one sees how difficult it is to press the analogy with astronomy. Competent astronomers might differ about what logicians call the connotation of the words 'heavenly body' but its denotation is comparatively fixed for them. Yet it is hard to say anything comparable about the relation between one theologian who is committed to belief in the "God of theism" and a colleague who is committed to the God above Him. They worship different Gods.

Such difficulties are bound to arise whenever a religious outlook which has come a long way from dogmatism and authoritarianism tries to achieve structure and vitality. It cannot formulate a catechism to be accepted by all who would teach in its institutions of higher learning, and yet it wishes to achieve a certain integrity and to invest its educational program with a degree of passion and life. Its association with a liberal university makes it hard for it to set up rigid, doctrinaire tests for its professors or definitions of the conditions under which religion must be studied. It has the problems of its virtues, and these problems are made even more acute if one conceives of religion as a total way of life. For in that case commitment means more than cognitive assent to the bare propositions of a theology; it also means acceptance of the attitudes, moral, esthetic, and social, associated with the religion in question. So that if the religion is a loosely knit rather than an authoritatively organized affair, the problem of determining a single sense of commitment becomes even more difficult. We are forced to such a degree of freedom in our conception of commitment as to make it possible for one so-called committed professor to be an agnostic in the eyes of another. Having come this far, why not go a daring step further?

Why not conceive of a divinity school which is part of a university, not as a school for instruction in one religion or family of religions, but rather as a school in which any of a number of rival religions are taught and defended actively by men who believe in them? In this way, I suggest, a divinity school associated with a large university will be able to overcome with integrity the difficulties I have already mentioned; in this way it will be able to bring itself into a viable and consistent relation with the spirit of the university as a whole. I realize that there are historical reasons which may make this impossible in the case of universities and divinity schools established or endowed under specific religious auspices, but I have warned the reader that I might be utopian. I now wish to begin the defense of my scheme by comparing the situation in a divinity school with that in a department of philosophy in a secular university, to which it is significantly similar.

The difficulties faced by a divinity school are not altogether different from those of philosophy when it comes to defining any minimum requirement for membership in the philosophy department of a secular university. And yet western, or at least Anglo-American, philosophy has achieved a certain degree of unity without commanding uniform commitment to specific doctrinal beliefs. Moreover, as only a cursory examination of western philosophy in the last generation will show, some philosophers believe that most of the questions which their fellow-philosophers debate are meaningless in a special sense of that much-abused word. What, then, can be *the* commitment which we require of a philosopher in the face of this welter of doctrines and points of view? — a welter, I should add, which is removed only by degree from that in which many theologians can find themselves even when they subscribe to the "same" religion. Can we transfer the philosopher's solution of this problem — for I believe it is a solution — to the case of divinity schools?

What is the philosophical solution? The required commitment of the philosopher is not to be measured by adherence to any fixed core of beliefs or doctrines of the kind that divide men into realists and nominalists, idealists and materialists, monists and pluralists, positivists and antipositivists. If there is any single required commitment it is to concern with *the problems* of philosophy, a dedication to them which can be and is shared even by those who spend so much time showing that these problems are meaningless, for they too are concerned with the problems. Professional philosophy in the secular tradition, therefore, is not a discipline in which one is required to hold certain canonical beliefs. It is rather a stubborn effort to deal with the problems to which different answers have been offered. Therefore a philosopher's only *required* commitment is to the pursuit of truth and understanding on certain topics.

My proposal for an ideal divinity school is that its professors be granted the same degree of freedom. One should certainly not demand commitment to a specific set of beliefs about God and then be satisfied with the most varied construals of the word 'God', construals which would allow theologians to disagree with each other fundamentally and radically while they gave the appearance of commitment to the same thing. That is literal double talk. In the divinity school which I have in mind theology would be defined in terms of its concerns and not in terms of its conclusions. The required commitment of the professor of theology would not be to a set of specified theological beliefs but rather, as in the case of the professor of philosophy, to an interest in certain questions and problems. And therefore if the problems of theology and religion should change, the commitment of its professors should change too.

The proposed requirement for a teacher of theology is in keeping with that sponsored by most of the other disciplines in the free, secular, modern university. Although I spoke earlier of astronomy as the science of heavenly bodies, it is not customary to regard such definitions of subjects as eternally binding. There was a time when mathematics was construed as the science of number and when physics was understood as the science of macroscopic bodies, but time has shown such definitions to be far too confining for the mathematics and physics of today. Moreover, it is exceedingly dangerous to imply that no one can practice a subject without believing in certain specified entities accepted at a certain period in the history of the subject. The problems associated with religion may vary, as the recent appointment of psychiatrist-theologians and the talk of a God above God both seem to demonstrate.

The implications of my proposal are, I suppose, radical. The ideal divinity school I describe would permit, indeed would encourage, as much richness and variety as possible. Not only would its professors expound and defend Judaism, Catholicism, Protestantism, and some of the less popular religions, but even agnostics and atheists might be given the opportunity to present their views. In this way a divinity school might emulate the freedom, the diversity, and the habits of controversy which characterize the rest of a great secular university. Unlike the undergraduate college, most of whose students do not enroll in order to be instructed in religion and whose faculty could not give such instruction successfully if it tried, the divinity school would be attended by students seeking the true religion and taught by professors who thought they had it. The common pursuit of truth under the instruction of those who differ, the competition of ideas and ways of life communicated in a scholarly way, would not only emulate the most attractive side of the modern university, but it might be a stimulant to creative religious and theological thinking. It might even help eliminate some of the tensions of our divided world, though I should hesitate to let its value depend on achieving that.

The faculty of such a divinity school as I project might wish to circumscribe the required commitment further. But any narrowing that sets the divinity school apart from the rest of the university as a place in which prescribed religious beliefs must be held by all of its professors is bound to create an unfortunate gulf between such a school and the rest of the university. The effect would be similar if any one of the departments of the university were to congeal itself into a center of ideological uniformity on subjects where competent scholars might differ. Naturally, there will always be many qualifications for a professor, notably excellence in the theology or history of the religion he teaches. And therefore at certain times, because of a lack of available talent, one might prefer to have no representative of a given religion on the faculty. Some philosophy departments have experienced similar situations in spite of strenuous efforts to avoid the congealment of which I have spoken. But in all such cases, whether a school or a department is involved, the decision as to whether the solid state has been reached should be in the hands of the faculty in question. Any one who is not arrogant enough to suppose that his own position represents final and immutable truth will wish to have distinguished colleagues who disagree with him, but he will consciously or unconsciously draw some kind of circle beyond which he does not look for colleagues. The astronomer no longer votes for alchemists, the psychologist no longer votes for phrenologists, and the philosopher, I hope, draws the line at obscurantism. In the case of the theologian the matter appears to be very difficult and I am in no position to say where he sets the limits of outer darkness.

In summary, I should like to say that the most obvious point of my argument is that the scholar who studies religion objectively need not accept the beliefs he analyzes or whose development he traces. Requiring him to be committed to these beliefs would be grotesque in the light of our experience.

The second and more important point is my proposal of a divinity school which shall be dominated by no one of the historical religions and which shall give a voice to all of them. In such a divinity school even a professor of systematic theology would not be required to assent to any previously specified set of beliefs. I hasten to add that I am not urging the requirement of noncommitment. That is to say, I am not arguing that professors in the divinity school I envisage should have *no* beliefs. I am rather arguing against the requirement of a core of uniform belief, and these are two different things. It is obviously necessary to distinguish between the assertion that one and the same view should be required of all scholars and the assertion that they all should have some point of view of their own. I deny the former but certainly affirm the latter. Creative work in any field is impossible without the adoption of a set of beliefs and attitudes and therefore it is not likely that a man who has no firmly held convictions or deep feelings about the problems of his field will come to anything, whether he be a theologian, philosopher, or historian. But the history of scholarship and teaching, especially in theology, has shown the danger of codifying and calcifying the doctrines that a man *must* hold. Every creative scholar does and should begin with certain basic beliefs and commitments, but any attempt to legislate what they should be is bound to imperil our scholarly tradition and educational system. In an effort to navigate between the extremes of uniform belief and no belief at all we should construe the required commitment of a professor in all parts of a free university — the divinity school included — in a way that transcends substantive belief. Such a commitment would imply no more than a serious, intellectually honest, dedicated concern with the problems of whatever subject he studies. If we demand more in the case of the divinity school, we separate its spirit from that of the rest of the university in a way that cannot be healthy. That is the moral of my utopianism.

Postscript

It has been said in response to the above argument (and in a less than utopian vein) that, after all, a divinity school is a professional school, devoted to the preparation of churchmen, and that if it were organized along the liberal lines described above, many churches would not accept its graduates. This may be a compelling argument to some but I am not moved by it. For if we believe in the principles of the modern secular university, we should reply: so much the worse for such churches. If they are not willing to allow their ministers to be exposed to a variety of efforts at reaching the truth on religious matters, they acknowledge their spiritual distance from the tradition of liberal education and scholarship. Suppose there were colleges which refused to give positions in philosophy to Ph.D.'s who had been exposed to a similar variety of doctrines in a graduate school of arts and sciences. Would we take this to be a commentary on the narrow-minded college or on the graduate school which held fast to its tradition of free inquiry? The question answers itself here just as it does in the case of the church and the divinity school.

10 ·

Original Sin, Natural Law, and Politics

1. *Credo and Non-credo.* Some years ago, in my book *Social Thought in America*, I reported on the declining reputation of American liberal thinkers like Dewey and Holmes, not realizing that I was noting a tendency that would soon swell into an effort to discredit totally the ideas of some of the most distinguished Americans of the present century. I still consider my criticism of Dewey and Holmes to be just, but the current intellectual atmosphere makes it plain that for all my reservations I have more in common with them than with most of their contemporary detractors. *Social Thought in America* is not the work of an empiricist turned transcendentalist, nor do I look back on it as the product of a temporary aberration. But recent events have brought the liberal outlook under a very different kind of attack. It should be said, therefore, that my book is in no sense to be identified with the more recent revivals of religious, conservative, and obscurantist thinking which have attempted to discredit and seriously lower the reputation of liberalism and secularism in social, political, and moral affairs.

To underline this I will consider in this essay the views of two distinguished critics of the liberal tradition: Reinhold Niebuhr, the most democratic and courageous opponent of secular liberalism on the American scene, and Walter Lippmann, who has bemoaned the disappearance of "The Public

Philosophy" in a vein distinctly antithetical to the outlook of Dewey and Holmes. In criticizing Lippmann and Niebuhr I mean to align myself spiritually with Dewey and Holmes, even though I am not always prepared to defend the actual letter of their texts. I do not share Niebuhr's faith, nor do I admire his Hegelian way of dealing with contradictions; I cannot accept the historical inevitability of sin which is such an important part of his view; I deplore Lippmann's revival of the ancient and obscure theory of essences and natural law. And, in general, it seems to me a sad commentary on American thought today that two of our most popular social thinkers can produce nothing more original or natural than original sin and natural law as answers to the pressing problems of this age.

2. *Niebuhr, Dewey, and Human Nature.* It is sometimes said that Niebuhr's reflections on human nature have provided a new generation of liberals with insights that transcend the limitations of Dewey. On the one hand Dewey is pictured as a disciple of the Enlightenment, confident of the intrinsic goodness of human nature, one of the latter-day *illuminati* who see man everywhere in the chains of ignorance and who hold that scientific knowledge will usher in a millennial era of social happiness through democratic planning. On the other hand Niebuhr is seen as a shrewd Pauline, aware of man's selfishness, and of his inevitable incapacity to free himself from the effects of original sin through his own unassisted efforts. Supplied with this more accurate picture of human nature, Niebuhr is supposed to see the folly of placing too much trust in any central group of social planners, while Dewey, it is argued, was ineffectually innocent, a child of light in

Niebuhr's Biblical phrase, but unable to illuminate this wicked world of gas chambers and mushroom clouds. Niebuhr becomes the symbol of tough, Christian realism, while Dewey represents soft-headed, complacent, dreamy, secular liberalism.

What we must consider, then, is the relation between Dewey's and Niebuhr's views of human nature, the grounds offered for them, and their political consequences.

Dewey is presumably a child of light, but what is a child of light in Niebuhr's view? He is defined by contrast to children of darkness "who know no law beyond their will and interest." By contrast "those who believe that self-interest *should* be brought under the discipline of a higher law could then be termed 'the children of light' "; the children of light "may thus be defined as those who *seek* to bring self-interest under the discipline of a more universal law and in harmony with a more universal good [my italics]."

Surely there is nothing wrong with being a child of light, then. To believe that one should bring self-interest under a more universal law and in harmony with a more universal good, is to act morally; and surely the effort to act morally is not being attacked by Niebuhr. One can hardly believe that he opposes the effort to bring self-interest under law, in spite of his grotesquely false statement that "nothing that is worth doing can be achieved in our lifetime." Therefore, one seeks for a more plausible explanation of what he means.

As we push on we see that Niebuhr may escape absurdity, but only at the expense of making it silly to say that Dewey is a child of light and at the risk of making the whole distinction between the two kinds of children useless. In the last analysis Niebuhr may mean by a child of light either (a) one who thinks it is *easy* to bring self-interest under law, or (b) one who thinks that we can bring self-interest *completely* under a higher law, that we will reach a time when men will *always* act so as to give only limited weight to their own desires. But on either view of a child of light, it is preposterous to suppose that Dewey is a child of light and doubtful to suppose that the contrast between children of light and children of darkness can illuminate the ideological struggles of our time. How can Niebuhr seriously represent his own version of the Christian view as the only one to navigate between idiotic optimism and equally idiotic pessimism, as if all rationalists and naturalists said that men were gods, while their opponents maintained that they were devils, and only Niebuhr knew the middle way? Dewey has never supposed that the way to social happiness would be *easy*, nor has he ever said that a time would come when *all* human action would be morally right and all tensions resolved. The following passage from *Human Nature and Conduct* may suffice to bring out the point:

In Aristotle this conception of an end which exhausts all realization and excludes all potentiality appears as a definition of the highest excellence. It of necessity excludes all want and struggle and all dependencies. It is neither practical nor social. Nothing is left but a self-revolving, self-sufficing thought engaged in contemplating its own sufficiency. Some forms of Oriental morals have united this logic with a profounder psychology, and have seen that the final terminus on this road is Nirvana, an obliteration of all thought and desire. In medieval science, the ideal reappeared as a definition of heavenly bliss accessible only to a redeemed immortal soul. Herbert Spencer is far enough away from Aristotle, medieval Christianity and Buddhism; but the idea re-emerges in his conception of a goal of evolution in which adaptation of organism to environment is complete and final. In popular thought, the conception lies in the vague thought of a remote state of attainment in which we shall be beyond tempta-tion', and in which virtue by its own inertia will persist as a triumphant consummation. Even Kant who begins with a com-plete scorn for happiness ends with an 'ideal' of the eternal and undisturbed union of virtue and joy, though in his case nothing but a symbolic approximation is admitted to be feasible.

It is true that Dewey in his later writings tended to identify the intelligent solution of a social problem as one that dis-penses with the use of force, and therefore seemed to imply that it was never desirable to apply force. If Niebuhr criticizes Dewey on this count, I can understand Niebuhr, but I reject another aspect of Niebuhr's attack on Dewey's attitude toward intelligence. Once we distinguish between the relatively spe-cific conclusion that all political problems can be solved with-out the appeal to force, and the more general philosophical thesis that no conclusion about the ways of achieving certain ends should be arrived at except by the use of intelligence or scientific method, we see a far more profound issue between Dewey and Niebuhr. In other words, if one identifies the use of intelligence with the use of absolutely peaceful methods, one is accepting a dubious thesis within political technology itself, but if one identifies the use of intelligence with the use of what is commonly called scientific method in the evaluation of judgments of political technology, one can only ask: What other ways are there? One must remember, of course, that we are thinking of political technology as the discipline in which we ask about the best ways of achieving certain social and political ends, and that answers to such questions are statements that a certain kind of action is most likely to achieve a certain kind of result.

3. *Human Nature and Politics.* So far, I see no reason to

think of Niebuhr as having demolished or replaced Dewey as a social or political philosopher. But we have not yet dealt with what is thought to be Niebuhr's chief distinction: his deeply "realistic" vision of man's state by comparison with Dewey's supposedly idle dreams. What can we say about this contrast after our earlier conclusions about Dewey's relations to the children of light?

Here it seems necessary to say, as one must so frequently say when one is bound by neither formula nor prejudice, that the differences which Niebuhr magnifies so dramatically and misleadingly are differences in degree of emphasis on the part of thinkers who see that man is not perfect. Some think that the resolution of social tension is extremely difficult and some are more optimistic; in short, there are disputes as to how heavenly earth can be. But can this bare, unqualified, banal dichotomy, if it is the real dichotomy between the children of light and the children of darkness, help us divide the intellectual or political globe in an interesting way? All we have here is the recognition that men are somewhere between the serpent and the dove, and while Niebuhr puts us closer to the serpent, Dewey puts us closer to the dove. But the serious question for political action is "How close?" in either case. Niebuhr's more recent reflections lead him to answer: "Too close to the serpent to allow for successful central planning," and for this reason some liberals who reject socialism in favor of Keynesianism now think of Niebuhr as one of the deepest political thinkers in America.

It should be remembered, however, that Niebuhr has not always held his present political position. He defended socialism in his earlier work, when he held the same Pauline and

Augustinian doctrine of man. What has happened since then is that Niebuhr's skepticism about man's power to help himself has deepened; Niebuhr has learned things about man and society which were not previously encapsulated in the view of man he inherited from Augustine and Paul. That view is consistent with a variety of political positions, and it is absurd to suppose that Niebuhr only recently began to wake up to "implications" that he should have seen in his salad days. Niebuhr saw Stalin, Hitler, Mussolini, and Franco in operation, and this, more than any theological speculation about man, must have brought home to him the dangers of limiting political freedom. In this respect he is like Dewey and all human beings who learn by experience. It is therefore wrong to say that while Niebuhr has a theory which permits him to see that man is not perfect, Dewey is tied to a philosophy which prevents him from seeing the same obvious fact. The difference between Niebuhr and Dewey must be put in more concrete terms and once we put it in this way we shall be leaving relatively empty "theories of human nature" for the solid ground of politics.

The contemporary liberal's fascination with Niebuhr, I suggest, comes less from Niebuhr's dark theory of human nature and more from his actual political pronouncements, from the fact that he is a shrewd, courageous, and right-minded man on many political questions. Those who applaud his politics are too liable to turn then to his theory of human nature and praise it as the philosophical instrument of Niebuhr's political agreement with themselves. But very few of those whom I have called "atheists for Niebuhr" follow this inverted logic to its conclusion: they don't move from praise of Niebuhr's theory of human nature to praise of its theological

ground. We may admire them for drawing the line somewhere, but certainly not for their consistency.

4. *Historical Inevitability and Original Sin.* Precisely because of the emergence of Niebuhr as an influence on so many
distinguished liberals of the present generation, there is a
greater need for some of Dewey's methodological exhorta-
tions. Dewey is committed to the use of empirical methods
in discovering what man is or is not likely to achieve, while
Niebuhr is, in the last analysis, a devotee of the *a priori* road
that begins with a theology based on faith. Furthermore,
Niebuhr is committed to a view of history which in its own
way is as rigid as any promulgated by Marx or the more dogmatic theorists of the Enlightenment. Niebuhr constantly
speaks of "the perennial and persistent character of human
egotism in any possible society," "the vast forces of historical
destiny," "inexorable historical developments," and of social
conflict as an "inevitability in human history," in a way that
leaves him open to all the arguments so powerfully deployed
by Isaiah Berlin in his essay, *Historical Inevitability*.

It is true that Niebuhr often shows a fondness for citing
historical evidence in support of his conclusions; he says, for
example, that the doctrine of original sin "emphasizes a fact
which every page of human history attests." But such evidence as he does offer is surely not enough to establish the
thunderous statement that man *cannot* conquer his selfish interests to the point of establishing a planned society. Niebuhr's dark view of man's estate is, in his own mind, a corol-
lary of his doctrine of original sin and that is a view of man
which, as he says in his *Nature and Destiny of Man*, transcends the canons of rationality. If history should fail to sup-

port his view, or if it should at any moment appear to go against it, Niebuhr's attitude toward his own doctrine would not be seriously affected, since his own conviction rests on faith. In this respect it resembles all of the interpretations of history, like Augustine's and Hegel's, which are demolished in Berlin's essay. But the matter should stand differently with those of Niebuhr's admirers who have not yet been persuaded of the theology underlying Niebuhr's reflections on history. How can those who are sober historians and who reject the pretensions of inevitability and necessity that they find in Toynbee or Marx, accept the block historical universe that Niebuhr portrays when he speaks of inexorable historical developments, vast forces of historical destiny, and inevitability in human history?

5. *From Kierkegaard to Hegel.* I have said little about the details of Niebuhr's theology, except to point out that it rests on faith and that it implies the inevitability of sinfulness in history. And although there is hardly space for dealing with the labyrinth of Niebuhr's theology, it is desirable to say something, however brief, about the inevitability of sin in Niebuhr's view, if only to remind some of his more agnostic admirers once again of what he says in his more theological writings. It is to Niebuhr's credit that he recognizes that "the Christian doctrine of sin in its classical form offends both rationalists and moralists by maintaining the seemingly absurd position that man sins inevitably and by a fateful necessity, but that he is nevertheless to be held responsible for actions which are prompted by an ineluctable fate." Relying in the most difficult spots on Kierkegaard, Niebuhr begins by asserting that man is both creature and creator, made in the

image of God and yet finite, caught in the necessities of nature and yet able to transcend them. Man's freedom creates the temptation to sin, and this produces his anxiety. His anxiety leads him to try to escape from finitude to infinity, to try to be God rather than to subject himself to the will of God. Lacking faith, man tries to establish himself independently, and by doing so, by giving his immediate necessities a consideration which they do not deserve, he loses his true self. This is why the sin of inordinate self-love points "to the prior sin of lack of trust in God." Man's anxiety arises out of his finiteness and his freedom, but when he comes to the fork in the road, he chooses the wrong path rather than the right because he has also committed the "prior sin of unbelief." And then all of the other sins come tumbling after. Finiteness and freedom *by themselves* would never lead to these other sins. The sin of unbelief is the extra factor and it, so to speak, lies behind the other sins of history. They are inevitable once we grant that we are doomed to be finite, fated to be free, and forced into unbelief. At best we can use our freedom to become aware of all this and to develop contrition, but even contrition is no permanent protection against slipping into the abyss that anxiety and unbelief prepare for us. Niebuhr says that none of this is to be taken "literalistically." He criticizes what he calls literalistic distortions of Christian doctrine, such as the view that we inherit corruption. This criticism is connected with Niebuhr's belief that we are not doomed to sin by *natural causes*, with his opposition to the Pelagian notion that original sin is a force of inertia in nature, and with his constant rejection of the view that man's *finitude* is solely responsible for his sinning. All of this Niebuhr expresses by saying that "evil in man is a consequence of his *inevitable though not necessary* unwillingness to acknowledge his dependence, to accept his finiteness and to admit his insecurity," and so it is important to say a few words on this contrast between the necessary and the inevitable, especially in the light of what was said earlier about Niebuhr's views on history.

The problem of necessity is one of the most difficult philosophical problems, and therefore one can never be sure of understanding even what the most clearheaded philosophers say on this subject. But there is a usage according to which what happens necessarily happens inevitably. Thus Webster, when he explains the meaning of "inevitable," quotes Burke as saying: "It was inevitable; it was necessary; it was planted in the nature of things." That is to say, we sometimes regard "inevitable" and "necessary" as interchangeable, even if as philosophers we are not altogether sure of what they mean. What, then, does Niebuhr want to bring out by distinguishing them? So far as I can see, that we do not sin necessarily in the sense of being determined by what he calls *natural* or physical causes, because we transcend nature. But Niebuhr says nevertheless that we cannot avoid sinning. His point is that we are driven to sin, not by physical events, but by other things which are equally beyond our control. Niebuhr therefore demarcates one kind of unavoidable act, that which is caused physically, and calls it a *necessary* one, while he calls another kind of unavoidable act — the kind produced by our finitude, freedom, and lack of faith — *inevitable*. The important point is, however, that he believes (a) that we commit evil acts which are unavoidable, and (b) that we are morally responsible for them, that is, subject to blame for them.

Now there have been philosophers who have tried to make the inevitability of an act consistent with praising or blaming it. And there are others like Professor Berlin, who think that inevitability and blame are incompatible. But Niebuhr is a very different kind of thinker. He agrees that there is a contradiction between them but, in his Hegelian and Whitmanesque way, accepts it. The doctrine of original sin, he says, "remains absurd from the standpoint of a pure rationalism, for it expresses a relation between fate and freedom which cannot be fully rationalized, unless the paradox be accepted as a rational understanding of the limits of rationality and as an expression of faith that a rationally irresolvable contradiction may point to a truth which logic cannot contain. Formally there can be, of course, no conflict between logic and truth. The laws of logic are reason's guard against chaos in the realm of truth. They eliminate contradictory assertions. But there is no resource in logical rules to help us understand complex phenomena, exhibiting characteristics which seem to require that they be placed into contradictory categories of reason." Some readers may appreciate what Niebuhr means when he adds that "loyalty to all the facts may require a provisional defiance of logic, lest complexity in the facts of experience be denied for the sake of a premature logical consistency," but how long does he want us to wait? With such a modest remark Niebuhr may disarm even some of the most logically hardened of his readers, but he can't help making them wince when he calls on Hegel's dialectic in his defense: "Hegel's 'dialectic' is a logic invented for the purpose of doing justice to the fact of 'becoming' as a phenomenon which belongs into [*sic*] the category of neither 'being' nor 'nonbeing.' The Christian doctrine of original sin, with its seemingly contradictory assertions about the inevitability of sin and man's responsibility for sin, is a dialectical truth which does justice to the fact that man's self-love and self-centeredness is inevitable. . . ." How easy it is for the extremes to meet and what an irony of history it is that a follower of Kierkegaard — the great enemy of Hegel — should have to appeal to Hegel to save himself at the most vital point in his argument.

6. *Enter Lippmann and Locke.* In turning from the thought of Niebuhr to the recent writing of Walter Lippmann we find a similar preoccupation with human deficiency, selfishness, and ineptitude, only this time the fault is said to lie not in power-mad leaders who plan us into totalitarianism but rather with the people, the masses who have secured so much power over government and turned statesmen into lackeys. In one respect, therefore, Lippmann and Niebuhr appear at opposite poles of the social thinking that has gained prominence since the work of Dewey and Holmes went into eclipse. Lippmann fears the masses and Niebuhr fears the leaders, so that while Niebuhr has replaced Dewey as the hero of some liberals who have abandoned socialism, Lippmann has come to replace Justice Holmes as the hero of the more conservative young men. Niebuhr uses the Augustinian doctrine of original sin while Lippmann appeals to the Thomistic concept of natural law.

The doctrine of natural law is one of the oldest and most debated doctrines in the history of moral and political philosophy. It is the central theory of the Catholic Church on moral and political matters; it was adopted by John Locke; it influenced the language and thought of the Declaration of Independence; it was rejected by Dewey, Holmes, and Veblen; it has recently been revived by many thinkers who, like Lippmann, cannot bear the absence of a set of moral principles which are universally binding, certain, rationally established by the inspection of universals, essences, or meanings, depending on which outmoded epistemology or ethics is adopted.

In holding certain "truths to be self-evident," the framers of the Declaration of Independence were speaking the language of Aquinas and John Locke. The latter, because he was so confused on the fundamental philosophical questions touching on the status of natural law, is one of the most *interesting* thinkers in the history of the subject. His position is central in the American tradition, and his own puzzlement reflects the philosophical problems surrounding natural law.

Aquinas believed that there are self-evident principles which, as he says, are those principles whose "predicate is contained in the notion of the subject," * and Locke believed that there are self-evident principles, which he explained as those to which we assent "at first hearing and understanding their terms," or those which "the mind cannot doubt, as soon as it understands the words." And although Aquinas and Locke agreed that there were self-evident principles, they diverged on the most important of all problems so far as natural law is concerned. In answer to the question: Are there any self-evident *practical*, i.e., *moral*, principles? Aquinas was quite consistent and answered affirmatively, but Locke wob-

---

* He added that "some propositions are self-evident only to the wise, who understand the meanings of the terms of such propositions."

bled in the most scandalous way. Sometimes Locke says that there are self-evident practical principles, viz., self-evident principles of natural law, and sometimes he denies that there are any self-evident practical principles. In a sense Locke's contradiction on natural law is the counterpart of Niebuhr's in the case of original sin; only Locke did not have the benefit of Hegelian dialectic.

I do not think that Locke saw this contradiction, but it should not escape the careful reader of his *Essay Concerning Human Understanding* and his *Second Treatise of Government*, both published in 1690. Locke tries to refute the belief that "there are in the understanding certain *innate principles*; some primary notions . . . characters, as it were, stamped upon the mind of man; which the soul receives in its very first being, and brings into the world with it." But an innate principle is quite different from a self-evident principle, according to Locke, and therefore he is not involved in any obvious inconsistency *here*, as some of his antagonistic critics have implied. It was perfectly possible, Locke thought, for a man who believed as he did that all our ideas arise out of experience, to hold that some true statements are self-evident. For example, the idea of red arises from experience, and the idea of green does; nevertheless Locke maintained that anyone who grasps these ideas, who understands the meanings of the terms 'red', 'green', and the others in the statement, 'Nothing which is red all over is green all over', will immediately assent to that statement. It is therefore self-evident but *not innate*.

Locke's blatant inconsistency consists in the fact that he says in the *Essay* that there are no self-evident practical principles but denies this in his *Second Treatise*. In the *Essay* he holds that so far from there being innate practical principles, there are not even any self-evident practical principles.

In the *Essay* Locke says:

I think *there cannot any one moral rule be proposed whereof a man may not justly demand a reason* [his italics]: which would be perfectly ridiculous and absurd if they were innate; *or so much as self-evident* [my italics], which every innate principle must needs be, and not need any proof to ascertain its truth, nor want any reason to gain it approbation. He would be thought void of common sense who asked on the one side, or on the other side went to give a reason why 'it is impossible for the same thing to be and not to be.' It carries its own light and evidence with it, and needs no other proof: he that understands the terms assents to it for its own sake or else nothing will ever be able to prevail with him to do it. But should that most unshaken rule of morality and foundation of all social virtue, 'That one should do as he would be done unto,' be proposed to one who never heard of it before, but yet is of capacity to understand its meaning; might he not without any absurdity ask a reason why? And were not he that proposed it bound to make out the truth and reasonableness of it to him?

It is puzzling after all of this to turn to his *Second Treatise of Government* and to find Locke saying that there is "*nothing more evident* [my italics] than that creatures of the same species and rank, promiscuously born to all the same advantages of nature and the use of the same faculties, should also be equal one amongst another." Now clearly this is a moral or practical principle: the telltale word 'should' indicates that. Therefore, according to the doctrine of the *Essay* many things are more evident than this natural law of equality; indeed, as we have seen, *all* self-evident *speculative* principles are more evident than it is. If it should not be obvious that Locke is contradicting himself we have only to read a little further on where he says with approval: "This equality of men by nature the judicious Hooker looks upon as . . . *evident in itself* [my italics], and beyond all question." What more do we need to show that the Locke of the *Essay* contradicts the Locke of the *Second Treatise of Government*, which appeared in the same year? The charge is simple: he at once affirms and denies that moral principles are self-evident.

7. *"They all go into the dark."* Mr. Lippmann is eager to revive the notion of self-evident natural law and to put it in the hands of wise statesmen who will not be so tied to the demands of the people. Presumably in agreement with Doctor Mortimer J. Adler, whose writing is favorably cited in *The Public Philosophy* and who has expressed similar views in a less winning way, Mr. Lippmann chastises positivist professors who have subverted natural law through a refusal to recognize that there is a realm of essences in addition to a realm of existence. It is ironical, therefore, that positivists like Rudolf Carnap have in recent times been the most active defenders of the notion of analyticity (the sister notion of self-evidence, as we have seen) as well as supporters of the view that meanings and universals exist. Positivists, of course, have used the notions of analyticity and meaning quite differently. They are mainly interested in showing that mathematical propositions are analytic, that is to say, true by virtue of the meanings of their component terms, and they vehemently (and laudably) deny that the principles of morality may be so viewed. But it is certainly wrong to say, as Lippmann does, that all of them deny the existence of the universals or meanings which are so essential for the philosopher of natural law.

In opposition to Lippmann, Locke, Aquinas, and the positivists, to say nothing of a vast number of the other philosophers, I think that the notion of an analytic statement, the notion of a self-evident statement as conceived by Aquinas and Locke, and the meanings so dear to all of them and Lippmann, are first of all obscure in themselves and secondly incapable of sustaining the philosophical load which has been put upon them. I shall concentrate on the significance of this contention for the doctrine of natural law, though I can at best outline only part of my view here.

Very few philosophers have taken the existence of meanings, conceived as universals, for granted. The usual pattern of philosophical argument is to assume that the reader believes in the existence of physical objects — the tables and chairs of epistemology books — but that he is too dull to see that universals like the attribute of being a table also exist. And so it is frequently pointed out that we couldn't understand the general word 'chair' unless it had a meaning quite distinct from every individual chair in the universe. In this way the existence of meanings or essences construed as properties of things is supposedly proven. But then a new move must be made, for the ordinary man has a rather limited conception of existence; in other words he uses the word 'exists' narrowly, as applying only to physical objects which exist in space and time, and this won't do. Having begun with a tolerance and a garden-variety understanding of the word 'exist', the ordinary man has now been led to the point where he must see that there are at least two meanings of 'exist' and that this is the solution to the problem of understanding. But can any one suppose that this postulation of Platonic meanings really illuminates the notion of understanding? We think immediately, and rightly so, of dormitive virtues "explaining" why opium puts people to sleep.

Does Lippmann really suppose that he can prove that there are essences which, if properly unpacked, make the truth of moral principles evident? Even if he were to accomplish the first bit of required persuasion — that is to say, even if the public should be persuaded of the existence of essences — it would be another thing to show them that the principles of political morality are self-evident statements about men in which, as Aquinas says, "the predicate is contained in the notion of the subject," or logically deducible therefrom. We know that Locke pleaded old age when he was asked to do this by his correspondent Molyneux, and there is a very touching letter to Molyneux in which Locke writes:

> The Gospel contains so perfect a body of Ethics that reason may be excused from that inquiry, since she may find man's duty clearer and easier in revelation than in herself. This is the excuse of a man who, having a sufficient rule of his actions, is content therewith, and thinks he may employ the little time and strength he has in other researches wherein he is more in the dark.

8. *Ethics without Essences.* The point is that all of this philosophical machinery is not so much an effective instrument for rational persuasion as for self-encouragement, useful for philosophical whistling in the dark. Having persuaded himself of certain moral principles and having discovered that some people in other places and at other times have doubted them, the weak man needs support. He needs to say that things in the realm of essence are so related as to substantiate or corroborate these principles of morality.

Now we all have deep moral convictions: we firmly believe certain moral principles which we try to act on to the best of our ability. They make up, along with others, the foundations of our whole structure of belief; they constitute our terminal beliefs. We want them to be consistent with each other and to fit in harmoniously and simply with other, less confidently held beliefs; we want this structure to mesh with experience and feeling. But individuals and societies have surrendered many beliefs which they once accepted as terminal, and some of these beliefs are moral beliefs. What, then, is the purpose in inventing a mysterious realm of essence *of which* our terminal beliefs are supposed to be true? Wouldn't it be saner to recognize that we all have our ultimate convictions at any moment, that they are not absolutely immune to change (though we can resolve, at our own peril, to make them permanently immune), that some people adopt the same beliefs as terminal and others don't? Who are the people we get along with? Very often the people with whom we have a great deal of agreement on these fundamental beliefs. Who are the people we quarrel with? Very often those with whom we don't share these beliefs. The point is that we and those whose logical lines end up at the same terminal shouldn't need the kind of mutual encouragement that comes from inventing a realm of essences beneath (or above) the terminal: and those who go in different directions are the last people in the world who are likely to analyze essences in the same way even if they agreed that such things existed.

I hesitate to assign all of this view to Holmes, but I think that it converges with what he says in his little essay "Natural Law." First when he says:

If . . . the truth may be defined as the system of my (intellectual) limitations, what gives it objectivity is the fact that I find my fellowman to a greater or less extent (never wholly) subject to the same *Can't Helps*. If I think I am sitting at a table I find that the other persons present agree with me; so if I say that the sum of the angles of a triangle is equal to two right angles. If I am in a minority of one they send for a doctor or lock me up; and I am so far able to transcend the to me convincing testimony of my senses or my reason as to recognize that if I am alone probably something is wrong with my works.

And also when he says: "The jurists who believe in natural law seem to me to be in that naïve state of mind that accepts what has been familiar and accepted by them and their neighbors as something that must be accepted by all men everywhere."

9. *Principles without Dictators.* As we have seen, in certain parts of theology Niebuhr may repair to the Hegelian dialectic too quickly and in others he may find it extremely difficult to beat a clear logical path to the world, but one cannot accuse him of the same sort of logical magic in discussing natural law. On that subject his view is deep and admirable, and he sees the antidemocratic potentialities of the doctrine even though it has been used by ardent democrats. Niebuhr decries Catholic as well as liberal confidence in natural law and shows the extent to which the doctrine can be twisted into special pleading and hypocritical justification of self-interest — especially when an institutional authority is set up as the custodian of morals. On this point Niebuhr's humility is encouraging even to those who cannot accept his theology. Niebuhr manages to give up "essentialism" in his theory of morality even though he maintains it in his discussion of original sin. After

seeing the defects of the philosophy of natural law, it is but a short step to giving up the whole effort to distill the essence of man. Yet Niebuhr fails to take it. For that reason the various Augustinian inevitabilities remain to plague Niebuhr even after the Thomistic necessities have departed.

By returning to Aquinas and Lippmann, we can see what Niebuhr means about natural law. Aquinas, as we have seen, says that some self-evident propositions are self-evident only to the wise, and Lippmann speaks of the principles of natural law as those which all men, "when they are sincerely and lucidly rational," will regard as self-evident. But who are the wise and the sincerely and lucidly rational? In practice the devotees of natural law identify them by their willingness to say that certain specific moral principles are self-evident. It is not as though partisans of natural law identify wise or rational men on the basis of a clear criterion independent of the specific principles that are said to be self-evident. On the contrary, to be a wise man according to Aquinas is virtually to be one to whom the moral principles are self-evident. This is most strikingly illustrated in Aquinas' statement that "to one who understands that an angel is not a body, it is self-evident that an angel is not circumscriptively in a place: but this is not evident to the unlearned, for they cannot grasp it." By similar reasoning some partisans of natural law must say that Justice Holmes couldn't possibly have understood what the term 'man' meant because he did not find the principle 'Every man has a right to live' self-evident. But consider what Holmes said on the point:

The most fundamental of the supposed pre-existing rights — the right to life — is sacrificed without a scruple not only in war, but whenever the interest of society, that is, of the predominant power in the community is thought to demand it. Whether that interest is the interest of mankind in the long run no one can tell, and as, in any event, to those who do not think with Kant and Hegel, it is only an interest, the sanctity disappears. I remember a very tender-hearted judge being of the opinion that closing a hatch to stop a fire and the destruction of cargo was justified even if it was known that doing so would stifle a man below. It is idle to illustrate further, because to those who agree with me I am uttering commonplaces and to those who disagree I am ignoring the necessary foundations of thought. The *a priori* men generally call the dissentients superficial.

It is ironic that while Locke believed in the self-evident principles of natural law his own attack on the doctrine of innate moral principles is a most profound statement of the dangers in the doctrine of natural law. He said:

It was of no small advantage to those who affected to be masters and teachers, to make this the principle of principles — *that principles must not be questioned.* For, having once established this tenet — that there are innate principles, it put their followers upon a necessity of receiving *some* doctrines as such; which was to take them off from the use of their own reason and judgment, and put them on believing and taking them upon trust without further examination: in which posture of blind credulity, they might be more easily governed by, and made useful to some sort of men, who had the skill and office to guide them. Nor is it a small power it gives one man over another, to have the authority to be the dictator of principles, and teach of unquestionable truths; and to make a man swallow that for an innate principle which may serve his purpose who teacheth them.

These words of Locke have more importance for us today than do all of his self-contradictory speculations about the natural law, for we live in an age that is crowded with dictators of principles who can read essences as easily as men used to read the stars. Whether one chooses to face them in the spirit of Dewey and Holmes or whether one chooses the faith of Dr. Niebuhr, is itself one of those ultimate questions which every man must answer for himself. In answering it and in settling upon his fundamental convictions, whether moral or metaphysical, a man will always run the risk of being called unwise, irrational, ignorant, or even mad by the dictators of principles. But this is not too great a price to pay for the liberty to think honestly and to act courageously.

ACKNOWLEDGMENTS

INDEX

ACKNOWLEDGMENTS

1. "The Social Role of Philosophy" was delivered as a public lecture at Tokyo University in the summer of 1952. It was printed in *Confluence*, vol. I, pp. 68–76 (December 1952) and later translated into Japanese under the title "Tetsugaku no Shakaiteki Shimei," pp. 3–17 in *Gendai Amerika no Kadai* (Problems in America Today), edited by Kishimoto Hideo, Tokyo University Press, Tokyo, 1954. A contribution to *Commentary* (January 1957) is interpolated.

2. "English Philosophy at Midcentury" originated as a talk on the Third Programme of the British Broadcasting Corporation in 1951. It was first printed in *The Listener*, vol. XLVI, pp. 590ff (October 11, 1951); reprinted in *Perspectives USA*, Pilot Issue, pp. 107–114; again reprinted in *Kenyon Review*, vol. XIV, pp. 599–607 (Autumn 1952). Approximately two paragraphs of it were reprinted in my *Toward Reunion in Philosophy* (Harvard University Press, Cambridge, 1956).

3. "Meta-meta-metaphysics" originated as a talk on the Third Programme of the British Broadcasting Corporation in the fall of 1957. It has never been printed before.

4. "Two Positivist Philosophers" is made up of two reviews, one of Richard von Mises' *Positivism*, which appeared in the *Kenyon Review*, vol. XIV, pp. 152–157 (Winter 1952); the other of A. J. Ayer's *Problem of Knowledge*, which appeared in *Encounter*, vol. VIII, pp. 80–82 (April 1957).

5. "Harvard's Philosophical Heritage" was first published in the *Harvard Alumni Bulletin*, vol. 60, pp. 161–164, p. 172 (November 9, 1957).

6. "A Plea for an Analytic Philosophy of History" was first published in Polish translation under the title "Filozofia historii w Ameryce" in *Kultura*, July–August 1953, pp. 173–182; in Dutch

translation under the title "Geschiedenisfilosofie in Amerika," *Amerikaans Cultureel Perspectief*, pp. 73–86 (Uitgeversmij W. De Haan N.V., Utrecht, 1954); in Italian translation as "La filosofia della storia in America," *Inventario*, Anno V, pp. 38–45 (October–December 1953).

7. "Historical Inevitability" appeared first as a review of Isaiah Berlin's book of the same title in *Perspectives USA*, no. 16, pp. 191–196 (Summer 1956); translated into French, *Profils*, no. 16, pp. 228–234 (Summer 1956); translated into Italian, *Prospetti*, no. 16, pp. 215–220 (Summer 1956); translated into German, *Perspektiven*, no. 16, pp. 214–221 (Summer 1956).

8. "Religion, Politics, and the Higher Learning" appeared originally in *Confluence*, vol. III, pp. 402–412 (December 1954); reprinted in abridged form in *The Ethical Outlook*, vol. XLII, pp. 115–119; reprinted in *Panorama*, vol. IV, pp. 40–48 (1955); reprinted in Israel Scheffler (ed.), *Philosophy and Education* (Allyn and Bacon, Boston, 1958).

9. "Religious Commitment and Higher Education" first appeared in *Confluence*, vol. VI, pp. 137–146 (Summer 1957); it was reprinted in Scheffler, *op. cit.*

10. "Original Sin, Natural Law, and Politics" was first published in *Partisan Review*, vol. XXIII, pp. 218–236 (Spring 1956). In considerably expanded form it was the epilogue of a reprint of my *Social Thought in America: The Revolt Against Formalism* (Beacon Press, Boston, 1957). I have reprinted the briefer version here because it conveys my views, in succinct form, on topics which are intimately connected with others discussed in the present volume.

INDEX